CONTENTS

S. Hrg. 107–1070

S. 2037, S. 2182, HOMELAND SECURITY AND THE TECHNOLOGY SECTOR

HEARING

BEFORE THE

SUBCOMMITTEE ON SCIENCE, TECHNOLOGY, AND SPACE

OF THE

COMMITTEE ON COMMERCE, SCIENCE, AND TRANSPORTATION
UNITED STATES SENATE

ONE HUNDRED SEVENTH CONGRESS

SECOND SESSION

APRIL 24, 2002

Printed for the use of the Committee on Commerce, Science, and Transportation

U.S. GOVERNMENT PRINTING OFFICE

90–267 PDF WASHINGTON : 2004

For sale by the Superintendent of Documents, U.S. Government Printing Office
Internet: bookstore.gpo.gov Phone: toll free (866) 512–1800; DC area (202) 512–1800
Fax: (202) 512–2250 Mail: Stop SSOP, Washington, DC 20402–0001

SENATE COMMITTEE ON COMMERCE, SCIENCE, AND TRANSPORTATION

ONE HUNDRED SEVENTH CONGRESS

SECOND SESSION

ERNEST F. HOLLINGS, South Carolina, *Chairman*

DANIEL K. INOUYE, Hawaii	JOHN McCAIN, Arizona
JOHN D. ROCKEFELLER IV, West Virginia	TED STEVENS, Alaska
JOHN F. KERRY, Massachusetts	CONRAD BURNS, Montana
JOHN B. BREAUX, Louisiana	TRENT LOTT, Mississippi
BYRON L. DORGAN, North Dakota	KAY BAILEY HUTCHISON, Texas
RON WYDEN, Oregon	OLYMPIA J. SNOWE, Maine
MAX CLELAND, Georgia	SAM BROWNBACK, Kansas
BARBARA BOXER, California	GORDON SMITH, Oregon
JOHN EDWARDS, North Carolina	PETER G. FITZGERALD, Illinois
JEAN CARNAHAN, Missouri	JOHN ENSIGN, Nevada
BILL NELSON, Florida	GEORGE ALLEN, Virginia

KEVIN D. KAYES, *Democratic Staff Director*
MOSES BOYD, *Democratic Chief Counsel*
JEANNE BUMPUS, *Republican Staff Director and General Counsel*

SUBCOMMITTEE ON SCIENCE, TECHNOLOGY, AND SPACE

RON WYDEN, Oregon, *Chairman*

JOHN D. ROCKEFELLER IV, West Virginia	GEORGE ALLEN, Virginia
JOHN F. KERRY, Massachusetts	TED STEVENS, Alaska
BYRON L. DORGAN, North Dakota	CONRAD BURNS, Montana
MAX CLELAND, Georgia	TRENT LOTT, Mississippi
JOHN EDWARDS, North Carolina	KAY BAILEY HUTCHISON, Texas
JEAN CARNAHAN, Missouri	SAM BROWNBACK, Kansas
BILL NELSON, Florida	PETER G. FITZGERALD, Illinois

S. 2037, S. 2182, HOMELAND SECURITY AND THE TECHNOLOGY SECTOR

WEDNESDAY, APRIL 24, 2002

U.S. SENATE,
SUBCOMMITTEE ON SCIENCE, TECHNOLOGY, AND SPACE,
COMMITTEE ON COMMERCE, SCIENCE, AND TRANSPORTATION,
Washington, DC.

The Subcommittee met, pursuant to notice, at 2:30 p.m. in room SR–253, Russell Senate Office Building, Hon. Ron Wyden, Chairman of the Subcommittee, presiding.

OPENING STATEMENT OF HON. RON WYDEN, U.S. SENATOR FROM OREGON

Senator WYDEN. The Subcommittee will come to order. Today, the Subcommittee on Science, Technology, and Space convenes the third in a series of hearings on improving America's homeland security through technology. We are also going to look in detail at two pieces of legislation, S. 2037 and S. 2182. It is my intention, working closely with my friend and colleague, Senator Allen and, of course, the chairman of the full committee, Senator Hollings, and the Ranking Minority Member, Senator McCain—it is our intention to work very closely with the Administration so that it will be possible at the next mark-up of the full Commerce Committee on May 16 to process both pieces of legislation.

I did have a very constructive conversation this morning with Mitch Daniels, the head of the Office of Management and Budget. He made it very clear that he wanted to work with our Committee on a bipartisan basis to address both of these important pieces of legislation, and I appreciate Director Daniels' constructive effort. We are going to work closely with the Administration so it will be possible to move these two important pieces of legislation, and I believe it will be possible to do that on May 16.

As this country mobilizes to protect itself from terrorism and other threats, a key weapon in our defensive arsenal is this country's great technological prowess. Many of the most promising technologies for improving security reside outside the government in the dynamic arena of private sector entrepreneurship, but the government can supply some key ingredients to make the technology sector's homeland security efforts more effective. Therefore, it is important to forge a strong partnership between the government and the technology sector in order to provide the best protection and response possible for the American public from high-tech cyber attacks to more conventional threats.

Many of the solutions for reducing this country's vulnerabilities are rooted in technology. Sophisticated hacker attacks on crucial computer networks must be dealt with by developing technology that can detect and prevent intrusion. More conventional low-tech threats like airplane hijacking likewise demand new technological responses. Better security screening and biometric devices are key to keeping terrorists off our planes, but when disasters do happen, technology can make a huge difference by enabling the first responders to communicate, by coordinating relief efforts to send resources where they are needed most, and by helping families locate loved ones.

Today we will look at two pieces of legislation, S. 2037, the Science and Technology Emergency Mobilization Act, which I am proud to have authored with Senator Allen, the Subcommittee's distinguished Ranking Member. This legislation seeks to provide an organizational structure to quickly locate and mobilize private sector scientific and technology expertise in times of crisis.

One pillar of that structure has been dubbed the National Emergency Technology Guard, or NET Guard. It would be a central part of a strategic technology reserve, much like this country's strategic petroleum reserve. The difference is, instead of oil the strategic technology reserve would be a deep well of private sector expertise and technological equipment that could be available around this country at a moment's notice.

The country's best scientific minds, technology experts, and technology companies would be invited to participate, and these companies, in my view, by helping to assist on a volunteer basis could make a significant difference. We envisage these volunteers becoming part of a NET Guard, and this country would have a central data base where we could catalogue the company's people and resources such as computers, software, wireless devices, and biohazard detection equipment, that would be available on a moment's notice.

The legislation has other objectives. One is to speed the evaluation of new products from the technology sector so that they can be matched with particular needs of federal security and response agencies. This seems to me to be particularly important, because with the federal government having been flooded with proposals, or various kinds of technologies, it is important that the government not buy outdated and antiquated equipment. This part of the legislation would make that possible.

The second bill the Subcommittee is going to consider focuses more on the direct threat to our technology infrastructures and the dangers posed by cyber terrorism. This is S. 2182, the Cyber Security Research and Development Act, which seeks to build a foundation of basic cyber security research, and grow the ranks of scholars who can devise innovative security defenses.

Since basic research is the soil out of which future cyber security advances grow, the government ought to support it. This legislation does so with a series of grants through the National Institute of Standards and Technology and the National Science Foundation. The awards are designed to encourage cutting-edge research today and to call more of the nation's brightest scientific minds to study the problem down the road. We are happy to have the opportunity to followup on our earlier work by examining and hearing testimony on legislative proposals with respect to both of these Senate bills.

I would also like to thank all the companies, organizations, and individuals whose support and input has been so helpful in moving both pieces of legislation forward. I want to reiterate my interest in working closely with the Administration on a bipartisan basis. Senator Allen and I have done that consistently throughout our service on this Committee, and I want to welcome my colleague and invite him for any remarks he would like to make.

STATEMENT OF HON. GEORGE ALLEN, U.S. SENATOR FROM VIRGINIA

Senator ALLEN. Thank you, Mr. Chairman. I want to begin by thanking you so much for calling this hearing on this subject matter, but in particular the focus on these two bills, S. 2037, the Science and Technology Energy Mobilization Act, and S. 2182, the Cyber Security Research and Development Act. I appreciate both your leadership and your cooperative spirit on these issues, and I look forward to working with you on it, and we will work with our colleagues—this is a bipartisan effort—and certainly Chairman Hollings and Ranking Member Senator McCain, as well as the Bush Administration, in working together for all of our shared goals in these regards.

I would like to thank all our witnesses for being here today, and in particular I do want to thank Mr. Jeff Logan from M/A–COM, Incorporated for testifying at today's hearing, and I look forward to reading your insights and all of your insights on both these bills.

Both these bills that will be the main focus of today's Subcommittee hearing highlight the vital role that technology plays in our nation, in our war to protect our homeland from terrorism, as we have highlighted, and I agree wholeheartedly with every remark that you made, Mr. Chairman.

And Senator Wyden, it's exactly my sentiments and philosophy in not just this hearing but in so many we have heard, whether in this Subcommittee, or as chairman of the Republican Senators High Tech Task Force, that there are so many technologies that are being developed or are actually currently developed that could help us in so many ways to save the lives of fire fighters, rescue workers, police officers, first responders.

There are technologies being developed, or are developed that can help us detect chemicals or radiological or biological agents. They also could improve and protect our communications systems from attack, and obviously the key from a lot of these is the interoperability of communications from all of these various federal, state, and local agencies prior to an attack, or during an attack, or if, sadly, it befalls us again, after an attack.

Now, S. 2037, the NET Guard bill, can play in my view a major role in preventing many of the problems that occurred during the attacks in New York City and at the Pentagon. The September 11 attacks taught us two things, one, how many technological improvements there are to help our security that are really, truly needed by our state, local, and federal services, and the second thing we learned from September 11 is that there is a great depth and reservoir of American goodwill to provide solutions.

I like the fact that this bill calls upon the ideas of the best and brightest minds of America's technology work force to act as an all-volunteer force to help restore communications and infrastructure operations after a major national disaster. Like all Americans, we had heard earlier in this Subcommittee and, indeed, the full Committee, of the heartening volunteer efforts of companies like Verizon, Intel, Accenture, Cingular, and others that volunteered both staff and equipment to restore communications in New York City and in the Washington, D.C. area, and this bill I think will be a way of helping facilitate their efforts without dampening any voluntary spirit.

Now, as you said, Mr. Chairman, there are many enterprises and commercial applications that can be adapted to meet governmental security or safety, public safety needs. I, along with Members—and I know Senator Edwards and everyone else has heard all sorts of ideas about companies, about products, their ideas, and how they will be able to help us, and every single one of them seems like a really good idea.

In fact, I was reading in the newspaper and found it interesting about ideas—this did not have to do with homeland security, but how to fight this war on terrorism, and there was one suggestion that the Bush Administration had received about how to get the Al Qaeda terrorists out of the caves, put in hives of killer bees, and I was thinking, you know, we have heard that is not a very high tech idea, but it gives you the idea of the breadth of ideas and at first you may laugh at that idea and say, you know, who knows, that might work.

The key, though—and I'm not suggesting we need killer bees for communication. I'm just trying to show you the breadth of ideas that we get as Senators, and I am sure the Bush administration gets, on how we could help.

Now, the key to all of this is to have a method of accurately testing and evaluating these ideas so that when procurement is going forward, or if somebody has an idea, there is a way to have that test bed, and that is something that I think is vitally important, and an important part of this bill, and I really look forward to making sure that gets achieved.

Now, the other bill in the Subcommittee that we are examining today, S. 2182, will address the important issue of cyber security. I will say that there is another cyber security bill that is not in this Committee, it is in Senator Lieberman's committee that Senator Bennett and others are pushing to make sure that there is the communication as far as cyber security, and I hope they will have a hearing on it. If you were in charge of that, we would have a hearing, but nevertheless, there are many concerns about our critical infrastructure in our country and the Internet. We have seen it in the past.

The survey just last year by the Computer Security Institute and the FBI found that 85 percent of 538 respondents experience computer intrusions. According to the Computer Security Institute and FBI survey, the estimated economic loss in these attacks was $378 million, a 43 percent increase from the previous year.

This Cyber Security Research and Development Act can, I believe, as you said, Mr. Chairman, play a major role in fostering greater research and methods to prevent future cyber attacks, and design more secure networks. The bill I think can very well harness and link the intellectual power of the National Science Foundation, NIST, our universities, and the private sector to develop new and improved computer cryptography and authentication, firewalls operations and control systems management and computer forensics.

I reviewed this bill, and the merits of it, and I would certainly be proud to join you as a cosponsor of the Cyber Security Research and Development Act. I think it is very much needed for our education and for our security, and again I look forward to hearing the testimony.

I will say, Mr. Chairman, I am on the Foreign Relations Committee and we are having a Top Secret briefing at 3 p.m. from Secretary Colin Powell on the Middle East situation, so I will have to read a lot of the testimony, but nevertheless we are going to work—although it will not be decided today. This is just one of those steps in the advancement of these good causes and good ideas.

Thank you, Mr. Chairman.

Senator WYDEN. I thank my colleague for an excellent statement, for working closely with us, and of course, we were talking about both these pieces of legislation as recently as 15 minutes ago, we are going to push very hard on a bipartisan basis with the Administration. I thank you for a fine statement and your leadership.

Now, I want to recognize Senator Edwards, who has been very passionate about his interest in science policy. We are so pleased to have him on this Subcommittee. What is so striking between the three of us, our states 30 or 40 years ago would not have had a whole lot of technology. They were largely agricultural states, and all of them now, in addition to growing things, something we feel strongly about, have made a big push in technology. Senator Edwards brings great expertise to this field, and we are pleased to have you here, and make whatever statement you choose to.

STATEMENT OF HON. JOHN EDWARDS, U.S. SENATOR FROM NORTH CAROLINA

Senator EDWARDS. Thanks, Mr. Chairman. I will be very brief. I think we are all very proud of the leadership that our three states have shown in the area of technology, and I am also proud, Senator Wyden, of the leadership you have shown in this area. Thank you very much for the work you have done, and my colleague from Virginia, thank you for the work you have done.

I think we all know that cyber terrorism and cyber crime rank among very serious threats to American security and safety. They are threats that ought to be addressed, need to be addressed. Last fall, I began working on some proposals to address these issues. We collected a lot of very good ideas from leaders in government and academia and the private sector, and in January I introduced two bills, the Cyber Terrorism Preparedness Act, and the Cyber Security Research and Education Act, and my hope, Mr. Chairman, is that we will be able to work together to make sure that our legislation accomplishes all the things that we are interested in accomplishing, and I want to just briefly highlight three points that I think we need to make sure are included in any legislation.

One, that we promote cyber security best practices. If you left your house without locking the door, you would expect to be robbed. Right now, government systems and private systems basically have a lot of their doors open. We need to change passwords regularly, but we do not always do it. We need to turn off certain dangerous computer applications, but we do not do it.

The legislation that I introduced would first encourage research and public education to develop and encourage best practices and, second, require government to adopt these best practices and move toward requiring them for government contractors and grantees. This should be a priority in any legislation that we move.

Second, we need to move some of the grant-making authority for cyber security research outside of the government. Government is full of terrific public servants, but the reality is that too often in this area we do not have the flexibility or the trust from the private sector that we need to lead in this area, so in our bill we propose funding a nonprofit, non-government consortium to do a lot of grant-making. I think that is an important component of any legislation we move forward.

And third, we want to encourage the development of cyber security experts in academia. Right now, the prestige in computer science is too often in other fields than cyber security. We need to get our best minds doing work that can protect our country and our economy. Our bill has a range of grants, fellowships, and sabbaticals for research in this field. I know that your legislation does the same thing. I think those are critical components of those bills.

So with that, Mr. Chairman, I would yield back to you, and thank you for the work you are doing, and the leadership you and Senator Allen have shown.

Senator WYDEN. Well, I thank my colleague, and we are going to work very closely with you. I think there are a lot of areas where there is common ground, and between now and May 16 we will work through the proposals you have, and the Administration's proposals, and we will move forward, and thank you very much for coming today.

We are also pleased to have Sherry Boehlert, an individual who has been a friend of mine for 20 years now, and we especially like the chance to partner with him. Chairman Boehlert, you have done a terrific job on the cyber security effort in the House. We appreciate your willingness to work with Senator Allen and I on the bill to mobilize volunteers in the private sector and science and information technology, and we are going to get both of these bills on the President's desk by working together and with the Administration, so you proceed as you choose to, and know that you have our welcome as usual.

STATEMENT OF HON. SHERWOOD BOEHLERT, U.S. HOUSE OF REPRESENTATIVES

Mr. BOEHLERT. Thank you very much. It is good to be back with friends, Senator Allen and you and Senator Edwards. I greatly appreciate your inviting me to testify today on the vital issue of cyber security, and I am pleased that our Committees have been able to work so well together. It is a critical matter. We are taking a bicameral, bipartisan approach to cyber security, the only approach that makes sense in dealing with such a massive, growing, and largely unappreciated threat.

Indeed, it would be hard to exaggerate our nation's vulnerability to cyber attacks. We rely more every day on an open network of computer systems for the most basic activities of our daily lives, communications, business transactions, and utility transmissions, to name just a few, and even our more secure systems have turned out to be porous when tested.

A computer attack by terrorists or common criminals or malicious teenagers, for that matter, could be monumentally disruptive and, indeed, life-threatening. So the obvious question is: What are we doing to prevent and prepare for such an attack? And, unfortunately the answer is just as obvious: Not enough.

The Administration deserves enormous credit for the work Governor Tom Ridge and Dick Clarke are doing to address this threat, especially in the near term. That is a full-time job to put it mildly. I think that we in the Congress have to spend some of our time helping to take the somewhat longer-term steps to counter cyber terrorism—even though we are not usually accused around here of long-term thinking. Still, improving cyber security requires a long-term commitment. Our adversaries are going to get more and more skilled, and we must get smarter and smarter to counter them. Like the Cold War, the war against terrorism must be won in the laboratory as much as in the battlefield.

With that in mind, I introduced H.R. 3394, the "Cyber Security Research and Development Act," late last year, and the House in February passed it by an overwhelming vote of 400 to 12. I am honored, Mr. Chairman, that you have introduced our bill in the Senate as S. 2182, and we have had some very promising conversations with other Senators of both parties, but I especially appreciate your leadership.

This bill directly attacks several problems that we have uncovered in testimony before the House Science Committee, and that I am sure you will hear about here today. First, the nation invests a pitifully small amount in cyber security research, and that is true of both government and industry. Government underinvests in part because no single agency has responsibility for the problem, and industry underinvests because the market has generally not put a high value on security compared with speed and price and other attributes of software.

Second, as a result of the minimal investment, few top researchers are engaged in cyber security research, and few students are attracted to the field.

Third, as a result of that minimal focus, our basic approach to cyber security has not changed in decades, even though it is known to be riddled with holes. Bill Wulf, the president of the National Academy of Engineering, and a leading computer scientist, calls this current cyber security paradigm a "Maginot Line" defense. That is not good enough.

So what does H.R. 3394 offer in response? It sets up programs at both the National Science Foundation and the National Institutes of Standards and Technology, two premier science and technology agencies. These programs will bring industry and academic experts together, fund new, more daring research, attract top researchers to the field, and recruit new students to the field. The legislation also tells NSF that it has the lead responsibility for eliminating our deficiencies in cyber security research. It is nice to know someone is going to be in charge.

In short, the new research grants, education grants, and fellowships created by H.R. 3394 directly address every problem we have identified that hampers our ability to develop a long-term strategy to counter cyber terrorism. As a result, the bill has been strongly endorsed by such groups as the Information Technology Association of America, and the National Association of Manufacturers and, indeed, by just about every leading high tech industry and academic organization. It has also been endorsed by the Administration, which I think is important to know.

The bill is a targeted, thoughtful approach to solve a problem that endangers our nation, and it reflects the advice of a range of experts from government, industry, and academia. I commend it to your attention, and I look forward to working with you to enact it and get it funded.

I also want to express my support for the thrust of your bill, Mr. Chairman, S. 2037, popularly known as "NET Guard." We are working on introducing it in the House. The bill addresses another serious gap in our cyber security preparedness—ensuring that we have the ability to respond should an attack actually succeed.

We saw after the World Trade Center attack just how important it was to get our communications and utilities up and running again, and Con Ed and Verizon and squadrons of volunteers did a magnificent job. It was little short of a miracle that the New York Stock Exchange was back in business so rapidly. We need to have a system in place to ensure that recovery can always proceed that quickly. That is the goal of Netguard, and we have to find the right language to ensure that we have the pieces in place to allow rapid recovery.

So Mr. Chairman, I look forward to continuing to work with you and with your colleagues to address this most difficult problem of cyber security. It is one that remains somewhat invisible to the public, just as the reliance on computer systems is somewhat invisible. If we do our jobs now, maybe the problem can remain invisible forever.

A note was just given me. Senator Allen has announced that he will cosponsor our bill, and that is a wonderful addition to the squad.

Senator WYDEN. Well, let me just say, Chairman Boehlert, you have given, as usual, just an excellent statement. I think you are absolutely right with respect to what you want to accomplish in S. 2182. I think, as you have stated, the Administration deserves substantial credit for their work on the legislation as well, and what it will do, what S. 2182 will do, is ensure that these two premier agencies, NSF and NIST, will have a permanent capability that will allow us to find those cutting edge strategies and technologies to fight terrorism, and I commend you for all your work. I thank you for agreeing to work with us on S. 2087, and since, Chairman Boehlert, you of course had the vote, let me just tell you a little bit of where we are and just sort of invite you to participate.

I think it is our desire on May 16, Senator Allen and myself, working with Chairman Hollings and Senator McCain, to have, with your input and that of the Administration, the ability of the Senate to move forward on both of these bills at the May 16 markup. Obviously, there are issues that we need to work on to ensure that there is no duplication and that we maximize the efforts to coordinate what is going on in the private sector with what is going on in government, but I think the pieces are falling in place.

Mitch Daniels, in my discussions with him this morning, was very positive in terms of working with us, and so we invite you and your staff to work with the Commerce Committee leadership on these issues. With a little luck, we will have both of these bills moving on May 16, and to a great extent that is possible, Sherry, because of all that you have done.

Mr. BOEHLERT. Thank you, Mr. Chairman. It is always a pleasure to work with you. We have a longstanding relationship. It is just nice, as the years pass, to get a little extra seniority and a little extra influence around this town, and we are putting it to good use.

Senator WYDEN. Well, you are using your gavel well, and we will try to complement what you are doing on this side. Unless you have anything to add, we will excuse you, but know that we are very appreciative of all your leadership.

Mr. BOEHLERT. Thank you very much.

Senator WYDEN. Our next panel is Mr. Ronil Hira, Institute of Electrical and Electronics Engineers; Dr. Lance Hoffman, Department of Computer Science, George Washington University; Mr. Jeffrey Logan, Business Development Manager, M/A–COM; and Mr. Wyatt Starnes, President and Chief Executive Officer of Tripwire in Portland, Oregon.

Let me also apologize, Dr. Strawn, I was reading from the wrong column. I apologize. We are very glad that you are here. Please, all of you, sit down and be comfortable, and we will make up for the omissions in the introductions, Dr. Strawn, by starting with you, and we will make all of your prepared remarks a part of the hearing record in its entirety, and if you could take 5 minutes or so and summarize your principal concerns, that would be great.

Dr. Strawn, welcome.

STATEMENT OF DR. GEORGE STRAWN, ASSISTANT DIRECTOR (ACTING), DIRECTORATE FOR COMPUTER INFORMATION SCIENCE & ENGINEERING (CISE), NATIONAL SCIENCE FOUNDATION

Dr. STRAWN. Chairman Wyden, thank you for the opportunity to testify at this hearing on homeland security and the technology sector, and on the cyber security research and development Act. I am George Strawn, the Acting Assistant Director for Computer and Information Science and Engineering at the National Science Foundation. Prior to coming to NSF, I was a faculty member in the university computer science department and the director of an academic computation center. As such, I have been concerned with issues like cyber security for a long time.

As you know, the Administration has yet to take a position on S. 2182, and so I will confine my remarks to the need for cyber security research and development and provide you with an overview of NSF's involvement in this important area. The Administration would appreciate an opportunity to analyze S. 2182 and submit written views on it prior to the Subcommittee's consideration of the bill. Cyber security is now understood to be a rather difficult problem. This is true for many reasons, including the fact that cyber security is the property of the total system, not system components, and those components include human and management elements as well as technology elements. This means that individually secure components and procedures can be put together and still comprise a system that is not secure, unless the proper attention is given to system level security considerations.

Of course, the fact that the Internet makes one big system out of millions, soon to be billions of IT components is a major source of complexity and insecurity. As you know, NSF focuses on long-term fundamental research and education in all areas of science and engineering. Long-term fundamental research has as its goal increased understanding of the subjects under study, and it has been the experience of science and engineering research that increased understanding leads to technology developments that are then put to important uses by a society.

We believe there are important reasons to increase the emphasis on cyber security research and development, that is, seeking a better understanding of cyber security, as NSF has recently been doing. A major problem in developing a robust cyber security research program is that the number of faculty members in academe doing research in cyber security has been quite small.

This is perhaps the most important problem to be solved as we seek to increase the amount of long-term fundamental research in cyber security, and unless there is a sufficiently large-size community of cyber security researchers, there will never be a sufficient number of graduate students trained in this field. This translates into a shortage of next generation cyber security workers and faculty. It also means we will continue to lack the courses and curricula needed to educate more students, undergraduates and graduates alike, for the cyber security work force.

Last September 5, NSF announced a new research program called Trusted Computing to focus our support for cyber security research. In addition to the estimated $20 million that we have been investing in cyber security-related research projects, we allocated $5 million for our Trusted Computing program. On December 5, we received about 120 proposals in response to that announcement requesting over $80 million of support.

Our expert panelists who reviewed those proposals rated almost half of them as worthy of funding. We believe that Trusted Computing program and similar programs will motivate more faculty to turn their attention and expertise to cyber security, and that this will help create a vibrant research community that will attack and ultimately solve many of the difficult problems associated with cyber security.

NSF also has considerable experience in supporting curriculum and academic program development and of administering graduate and undergraduate trainee programs such as scholarships for service, the Cyber Corps program. This program has been funded at approximately $11 million for the past 2 years, and the Administration is requesting $19.2 million in supplemental funding to enhance the program in fiscal year 2002.

Such activities also help accelerate developments in cyber security, especially when coupled with vibrant research support to attract research faculty into the area, as mentioned above.

Thank you again for the opportunity to testify, and I would be happy to respond to any questions you may have.

[The prepared statement of Dr. Strawn follows:]

PREPARED STATEMENT OF DR. GEORGE STRAWN, ASSISTANT DIRECTOR (ACTING), DIRECTORATE FOR COMPUTER INFORMATION SCIENCE & ENGINEERING (CISE), NATIONAL SCIENCE FOUNDATION

Chairman Wyden, Senator Allen, Members of the Committee, thank you for the opportunity to testify at this hearing on Homeland Security and the Technology Sector and the Cyber Security Research and Development Act. I am George Strawn, acting Assistant Director for Computer and Information Science and Engineering at the National Science Foundation. Prior to coming to NSF, I was a faculty member in a University Computer Science department and the director of an Academic Computation Center. As such I have been concerned about issues such as cybersecurity for a long time. As you know, the Administration has yet to take a position on S. 2182 so I will confine my comments to the need for cybersecurity R&D and provide you with an overview of NSF involvement in this important area. The Administration would appreciate an opportunity to analyze S. 2182 and submit written views on it prior to the Subcommittee's consideration of the bill.

Although cybersecurity has always been an important part of information technology (IT), over the last decade its importance has been greatly magnified. This is so because IT systems and services now are pervasive throughout society and because the Internet now ties together so many of our IT systems. While this interconnectedness of IT systems is enabling great productivity gains for the U.S. economy, it has also enabled great gains for IT mischief makers and outlaws. Clearly, there is much understanding yet to be gained if we are to avoid unpleasant surprises and to foil those who would attack the internet or use it for illegal purposes.

Although the defense sector has always paid great attention to cybersecurity, the same cannot be said about many civilian applications of IT. Until recently, cybersecurity has been considered an "optional add-on" for many IT systems. As recently as two years ago, discussion at a President's IT Advisory Committee (PITAC) meeting indicated that the private sector "was not being rewarded" for cybersecurity products and services because they made IT systems more complicated and slower at a time when customers were wanting more simplicity and speed. Although these circumstances have begun to change, there is much to do before we will be able to achieve desired levels of cybersecurity.

Cybersecurity is now understood to be a rather difficult problem. This is true for many reasons, including that fact that cybersecurity is a property of the "total system", not of the system components (and those components include human and management elements as well as technology). This means that individually secure components and/or procedures can be put together to comprise a system that is not secure—unless the proper attention is given to system-level security considerations. Of course, the fact that the Internet makes "one big system" out of millions (soon to be billions) of component IT systems is a major source of complexity and insecurity.

Early research and development work on the Internet, as with many IT developments of the past, focused on "making it work", not necessarily on making it secure. And because cybersecurity is a systems property, trying to add it on as an afterthought is very problematic. It would be much better to recreate IT systems with cybersecurity as a major design criteria than to attempt to patch it in after the fact.

Of course, we must and can attend to short-term needs and to long-term improvements simultaneously. Short-term cybersecurity patches are not only possible but are in progress throughout the IT world. In fact, a major challenge is to get cybersecurity services and procedures that have been developed over the last few years into wide use. Although there may be useful tactical contributions to cybersecurity that NSF can make (such as cybersecurity emphases in our Digital Government program), I would like to focus on longer term issues in cybersecurity because that is where NSF's contributions can be the greatest.

As you know, NSF focuses on long-term fundamental research and education in all science and engineering disciplines. This long-term fundamental research has as its goal increased understanding of the subjects under study. And it has been the experience of science and engineering research that increased understanding leads to technology developments that are then put to important uses by society. In many cases the societal uses that result from scientific understandings were not apparent at the time the scientific work was being done. For example, important applications to cybersecurity may arise out of scientific research in IT systems (or even in other sciences) that doesn't initially appear to be related to security. Nevertheless, there are important reasons to increase the emphasis on cybersecurity R&D as NSF has recently been doing.

NSF has supported cybersecurity research for a number of years, recently at a level of approximately $20 million. A major problem in developing a robust cybersecurity research program is that the number of faculty members doing research in cybersecurity has been quite small. This is perhaps the most important problem to be solved as we seek to increase the amount of long term fundamental research in cybersecurity. Unless there is a sufficiently large-size community of cybersecurity researchers, there will never be a sufficient number of positions for graduate students to assist in the conduct of that research. This translates into a shortage of next-generation cybersecurity workers and faculty. It also means we will lack the courses and curricula needed to educate more students—undergraduates as well as graduates—ready to go into the cybersecurity workforce.

NSF's Scholarships for Service/Cybercorp program is one way we are trying to address this issue. This program makes awards to qualified institutions to provide scholarships to undergraduate and graduate students studying computer security. In exchange, the recipients must serve in the federal government for at least two years. The program also provides capacity building grants to improve the quality and increase the production of computer security professionals. The program has been funded at approximately $11 million the past two years and the Administration is requesting $19.3 million in supplemental funding to enhance this program in FY 2002.

Last September 5th, NSF announced a new research program, Trusted Computing, to focus our support for cybersecurity research. In addition to the estimated $20 million that we anticipate as our ongoing investment in distributed cybersecurity research projects, we allocated an additional $5 million for the Trusted Computing program. On December 5th, we received about 120 proposals in response to that announcement requesting over $80 million of support. Our expert panelists who reviewed those proposals rated about 10 percent of them as "highly competitive" (high praise from the ever-critical research community) and rated almost half of them as worthy of funding. We will award funding to the highly competitive proposals. We believe that this program will motivate more faculty to turn their attention and expertise to cybersecurity. It will be necessary to focus attention on programs like Trusted Computing over the next several years if we are to help create a vibrant research community that will attack, and ultimately solve, many of the difficult problems associated with cybersecurity.

In addition to individual research awards, NSF has recently increased the number of large project interdisciplinary awards it has made in areas of IT research. Under the Information Technology Research (ITR) priority area initiated in 2000, NSF began a major invigoration of its IT research activities, including a focus on large, interdisciplinary research projects. We believe that this focus has already begun to show extremely valuable results by enabling computer scientists and engineers to work collaboratively on problems that require expertise from many areas to solve. I believe that many cybersecurity problems will also benefit from interdisciplinary groups or centers working collaboratively on their solutions. One important goal of fundamental long term research in cybersecurity will be to produce agreement on what, in fact, constitutes as secure system. When such an agreement is in hand, it will be possible to formulate important cybersecurity standards that, like all important standards, will facilitate their realization.

NSF also has considerable experience in supporting curriculum and academic program development and of administering graduate traineeship programs. Such activities could also help accelerated academic developments in cybersecurity as long as they are coupled with vibrant research support to attract the research faculty into the area as mentioned above.

NSF focuses on people, ideas, and tools as it pursues its goals of helping to keep the U.S. in a world-leadership position in science and engineering research and education. Increasingly IT tools and services are required by all academic disciplines to achieve these goals. Therefore our efforts to contribute to cybersecurity research and development are increasingly required for our science and engineering community as well as by society at large. As IT continues to transform society, cybersecurity continues to increase in importance and is of increasing priority on our list of important scientific and engineering activities.

Thank you again for the opportunity to testify, and I would be happy to respond to any questions you may have.

Senator WYDEN. Very good. Let us move on now to Dr. Hoffman.

STATEMENT OF DR. LANCE HOFFMAN, DEPARTMENT OF COMPUTER SCIENCE, THE GEORGE WASHINGTON UNIVERSITY

Dr. HOFFMAN. Thank you, Chairman Wyden. It is an honor to have this opportunity to appear before you today to comment on S. 2037, the Science and Technology Emergency Mobilization Act, and S. 2182, the Cyber Security Research and Development Act. My name is Lance Hoffman. I am professor of computer science at the George Washington University here in Washington, D.C., where I lead the computer security graduate program in computer science. I am a fellow of the Association for Computing Machinery, the ACM, an organization of 75,000 computer professionals with active professional and student chapters in Oregon, Virginia, and most states throughout the nation.

This statement today has been endorsed by the ACM's Committee on Computer Security and Privacy and the U.S. Public Policy Committee of the ACM, the USACM. I will summarize it in the interest of time. My entire statement has been submitted for the record.

First, let me address S. 2182. This bill takes important steps to develop the cadre of scientists, engineers, and computer specialists who understand current information assurance problems and can ameliorate them while also developing long-term solutions based on improved, smarter technologies. It does this by new research and education programs at the National Science Foundation and the National Institutes of Standards and Technology.

Computer security and information assurance have had trouble in the past competing with more established disciplines. Students and faculty have been driven by available funding opportunities to work on problems that are better known and whose solutions are in some cases more developed, but less important and critical to the nation than the security of its infrastructure. This bill will help remedy that situation.

I especially like the inclusion of privacy and vulnerability assessments, also known as risk analysis, as important areas of study, since innovative technical solutions will fail if they do not take into consideration the surrounding constraints. These constraints include politics, cost, legal liability, and other technologies like battery life.

I very much support the bill. The Committee may wish to consider a few minor improvements. First of all, there is an intense nation-wide competition for the current small number of recent Ph.D graduates interested in a faculty position in computer security and information assurance. Explicitly allowing funds for faculty recruitment from outside, for example, from retirees, might provide another source of qualified people to buildup the training cadre more rapidly.

Second, program managers at NIST and NSF should be allowed a bit more discretion in funding extraordinary projects with high risk and high potential. Setting aside a small percentage of the funds of this bill for innovative projects that address evolving and emergency research issues will allow researchers to fund a planning workshop or encourage an add-on specialty day at an existing conference in a hurry, without encountering a lot of red tape.

Finally, I respectfully suggest that universities be allowed to concentrate first on curriculum development and student recruitment. Later, universities could be required to collect appropriate placement data from students as they exit the program. The bill as written I believe currently requires placement data up front, and I think this competes with getting these new programs off to a good start.

Let me now turn to S. 2037. S. 2037 establishes pilot programs aimed at achieving the interoperability of communications systems used by emergency response agencies. It is good as far as it goes,but it is incomplete. It is also necessary to improve the integrity, assurance, and security of these systems. Standards bodies, including NIST, should work to develop better wireless standards to ensure security and utility of such systems.

Also, while this legislation takes necessary steps to require expertise checks, it lacks similar safeguards requiring background checks, potentially allowing the introduction of technically competent, malevolent individuals into the nation's infrastructure defense. We must verify both the technical credibility and the personal background of individuals selected for the National Emergency Technology Guard that is envisioned in this bill.

A final point. If and when utilized, the virtual technology reserve data base should only be used, and not misused by those responsible. The data base must be designed and tested properly and vetted by experts in data bases, privacy, and security.

A final word on the chilling effects of the Digital Millennium Copyright Act. I would be remiss if I did not mention these. The DMCA's restrictions have the potential to cripple the very security advancements that S. 2037 and S. 2182 are intended to generate, and its limited exemptions have not provided a safe harbor for researchers. I urge you to reexamine it and similar laws.

Thank you, Mr. Chairman, for the opportunity to appear before you today. I would be pleased to answer any questions you might have.

[The prepared statement of Dr. Hoffman follows:]

PREPARED STATEMENT OF DR. LANCE HOFFMAN, DEPARTMENT OF COMPUTER SCIENCE, THE GEORGE WASHINGTON UNIVERSITY

Thank you, Chairman Wyden, Senator Allen, and other distinguished members of the Science, Technology, and Space Subcommittee. It is an honor to have this opportunity to appear before you today and to assist in your efforts to strengthen our nation's information infrastructure and improve our capability to respond and recover from terrorist attacks and other emergencies.

I am Lance J. Hoffman, Professor of Computer Science at the George Washington University here in Washington, D.C. I lead the computer security graduate program in computer science and the Computer Security and Information Assurance Graduate Certificate Program. This academic year, I taught information policy and information warfare courses to students of computer science, international affairs, political science, and other fields. In 1993, I founded the School of Engineering's Cyberspace Policy Institute to examine the relationship between the technical and other factors that affect security, privacy, and related aspects of computer and information systems.

I am a Fellow of the Association for Computing Machinery (ACM), the nation's oldest and largest professional society of computer scientists, educators and other computer professionals committed to the open interchange of information concerning computing and related disciplines. The ACM has 75,000 individual members, including active professional and student chapters in Oregon, Virginia, and most states throughout the nation.

To underscore the importance of today's hearing this statement has been endorsed by the ACM's Committee on Computer Security and Privacy and the U.S. Public Policy Committee of the ACM (USACM).

I appreciate this opportunity to comment on S. 2037, the Science and Technology Emergency Mobilization Act, and S. 2182, the Cyber Security Research and Development Act, two significant pieces of legislation designed to address our nation's information assurance needs.

S. 2182

First, let me address S. 2182. This bill takes important steps to develop the cadre of scientists, engineers, and computer specialists who understand current information assurance problems and can ameliorate them while also developing long-term solutions based on improved, smarter technologies. To date, despite the fact that an increasing amount of daily life involves reliance on computer systems and networks, there is a remarkably small amount of long-term, ongoing funding available for computer security and information assurance research and development designed to solve these problems. This bill may remedy these concerns by providing the incentives and human resources necessary to meet some of today's security challenges and to take on tomorrow's. It does this in several ways, notably by the new research and education programs it calls for at the National Science Foundation (NSF) and the National Institute of Standards and Technology (NIST).

These programs will promote more innovative research in information assurance by attracting technically competent researchers into this field of national need. The bill is written in such a way that everyone from a senior faculty member wishing to focus his or her attention on computer security to a bright undergraduate student will be encouraged to work in this field. It will help to address the critical shortage of Ph.Ds and graduates in the security field that limits opportunities for research and solving the critical challenges we face.

Computer security and information assurance have had trouble in the past competing with more established disciplines. Students and faculty have been driven by available funding opportunities to work on problems that are better known and whose solutions are in some cases more developed, but less important and critical to the nation than the security of its infrastructure. This bill will help to remedy that situation.

I especially like the inclusion of privacy and risk analysis as important areas of study, in addition to what some might consider more purely technical areas. Since innovative technical solutions developed in a vacuum without taking into consideration the surrounding constraints related to politics, cost, and legal liability will fail, the inclusion of these areas will guarantee that the pure technological solutions that come out of the programs that this bill funds will actually have a good chance of being implemented, working, and ultimately improving the security of the nation's infrastructure.

I also appreciate the foresight of the bill in recognizing and supporting not only traditional undergraduate and graduate fields of study, but also certificate programs in the area. I direct a certification program where working professionals come in after a full day at work, and devote an additional five hours toward a certification in security and information assurance. In the program we have just started, more than a quarter of the students have been motivated to go back to school and pursue more advanced master's and doctoral studies in this area, and to apply the graduate credits earned with their certificate to those higher degrees.

The bill is excellent as written, but the Committee may wish to consider a couple of minor changes that would improve it even further. For instance, it currently provides funds for faculty retraining in this area. But in many cases, this may not be a viable option since many universities are stretched thin in trying to properly cover the currently recognized core areas of computer science. It is hard enough to get established faculty members in one field to change specialties, and recruiting across departments is almost impossible.

There are only a limited number of faculty members in the U.S. who have significant background in security research. As my colleague Professor Eugene Spafford of Purdue University pointed out in his testimony last fall to the House Committee on Science, an informal survey of 23 preeminent U.S. universities with information security programs found that they graduated a combined total of 20 Ph.Ds in security over the last three years. As you can imagine, there is an intense competition for the even smaller number of graduates interested in a faculty position. Explicitly allowing funds for faculty recruitment from outside (for example, from retiring federal government and contractor security experts who have appropriate credentials, teaching skills, and the motivation to work as part-time or full-time faculty but would not otherwise have the opportunity) might provide another solution to this problem of building up the training cadre more rapidly.

While I am very encouraged with the funds authorized by this legislation, I would also suggest that program managers at NIST and NSF be allowed a bit more discretion in funding extraordinary projects with high risk and high potential. Setting aside a small percentage of the funds of this bill for small, innovative projects that address evolving and emerging research issues will allow researchers to, for example, fund a planning workshop or to encourage an add-on specialty day at an existing conference without a lot of red tape. These opportunities for research and information dissemination may lead to new innovative solutions and other advances in information security.

My final remark on S. 2182 relates to the requirement for placement data in fields related to computer and network security. A study of potential enrollment and placement for students enrolled in a proposed computer and network security program may be hard for many universities to generate at the same time they are starting these programs and assimilating the additional students generated by this and other programs. As a result, the development and growth of these programs could be unnecessarily impeded. I respectfully suggest that universities be allowed to concentrate on curriculum development and student recruitment up front. If you wish, universities could be required to collect appropriate placement data from students as they go through and exit the program. But requiring this up front is counterproductive.

S. 2037

Turning my attention to S. 2037, the Science and Technology Emergency Mobilization Act, I wish to commend the members of this Subcommittee for their noble attempt to harness the outstanding capabilities of our nation's science and technology community, especially in times of national crisis. Faced with the realities of September 11, many members of the computing community wished to provide their technical assistance towards safeguarding our nation's infrastructure and in recovering from the attacks. S. 2037 would provide opportunities to match security experts where their services are most needed.

I wish to offer the following recommendations to build upon the many fine provisions of S. 2037. First, in establishing pilot programs aimed at achieving the interoperability of communications systems used by emergency response agencies, it is also necessary to achieve the integrity, assurance, and security of the communications. In attempting to improve emergency communications, it would be shortsighted to sacrifice security to achieve utility, particularly if it leads to vulnerable emergency communication systems. Wireless standards, where they exist, are known to be weak. Standards bodies, including NIST, should work to develop better wireless standards to ensure security and utility of such systems.

While the legislation takes necessary steps to require expertise checks, it lacks similar safeguards requiring background checks. This vulnerability might allow the introduction of technically competent malevolent individuals into risk equation. If we don't verify both the technical credibility and the personal background of individuals, we risk doing more harm than good.

Authentication precautions and other security mechanisms, combined with privacy policy guidelines, will be necessary so that if and when utilized, the "virtual technology reserve" database is only used by those responsible and is not misused (e.g., by an enemy attacking using a form of information warfare and polluting the database or identifying and harassing or impeding the responders identified therein).

The database will need to be designed and tested properly; possibly using competing designs with rapid prototyping. Both database and security experts should work on system design to insure appropriate access and security balances, speed of responsiveness, update ability, and accuracy.

While S. 2037 will help our nation respond to acts of terror and other emergencies, we must simultaneously engage in a more proactive approach that focuses on prevention. "Emergency prevention and response" is stated as an objective but it is much easier to demonstrate response than prevention [it's hard to have a demonstration if nothing is happening].

Chilling Effects of the Digital Millennium Copyright Act

One last but critical point that I wish to leave you with is that laws like the Digital Millennium Copyright Act (DMCA) inhibit the ability of individuals to engage in critical research in computer security and related fields. Unfortunately, this has certain implications for national security. For instance, researchers who study or teach encryption, computer security, or otherwise reverse engineer technical measures and who report the results of their research in this area face new risks of legal liability under the DMCA. As University of California at Berkeley Law Professor Pamela Samuelson has noted, the limited exemptions carved-out in the DMCA have been found to be of little value to the research community. I encourage you to reexamine laws that prohibit or restrict computing technology instead of undesirable behavior. DMCA-like restrictions have the potential to cripple the very security advancements S. 2037 and S. 2182 are intended to advance.

In summary, I commend the members of the subcommittee for their legislative efforts to enhance the security of our nation's infrastructure and our ability to respond to national emergencies. Thank you for the opportunity to appear before you today. I would be pleased to answer any questions you might have.

Senator WYDEN. Dr. Hoffman, thank you. I think the DMCA proposal may be a little much for us to get into in legislation that we would like to have moving in a month or so, but I think you know we very much value the work you are doing, and your organization. We will have some questions in a moment. We would welcome Mr. Starnes, and we are glad once again Oregon is pioneering in this area, and we welcome you, Wyatt, and you may proceed.

STATEMENT OF W. WYATT STARNES, PRESIDENT AND CHIEF EXECUTIVE OFFICER, TRIPWIRE, INC.

Mr. STARNES. Thank you, Mr. Chairman. My name is Wyatt Starnes, founder and CEO and president of Tripwire, Incorporated. I would like to start by commending this Subcommittee, led by Senator Wyden, Senator Allen, and their staff in directing focus on critical issues of cyber security. I appreciate the opportunity to testify orally before the Committee today. I have also submitted expanded written comments for the record.

For the past decade, the technology that is Tripwire has focused on data integrity assurance as a means to achieve higher levels of security, control, availability, and reliability of computing systems. Our focus has been on protecting critical computing infrastructure within the commercial and government sectors.

Tripwire software has been deployed on hundreds of thousands of critical systems worldwide, including many in this building. It is as an information security professional and a business leader, as well as a citizen, that I am here before you today to discuss the security and control of our nation's cyber infrastructure, and why I've concluded that both Senate Bill 2182, the Cyber Security Research and Development Act, as well as Senate Bill 2037, the Science and Technology Emergency Mobilization Act, represent very positive steps forward to safeguard our nation's somewhat fragile digital infrastructure.

The development of Tripwire's technology was supported entirely with commercial funding as a part of Purdue's center-based long-term research efforts, which have no federal support. They are almost entirely funded by corporate contributions. Recently, market pressures, including the economic downturn, have put a damper on commercial funding, reducing the capacity of many academic programs. It may even threaten the existence of a few at a time when they are just beginning to realize their full value.

We support Senate Bill 2182 as it provides a means to address these issues by creating and funding programs to stimulate new cyber research and development. They should help to prime the pump, enhancing our ability to stay ahead in the development of critical cyber protection technologies. The problem, however, extends beyond federal funding issues. We must enhance the coordination among the state-federal government as well as the academic community and private industry.

As a CEO of a commercial company, I routinely see the desire and need for government and commercial entities to enhance their security procedures, in many cases especially within the government sector. These requirements come months, or even years before the funding becomes available. It is in these critical gaps that our cyber vulnerability as a nation is the greatest. Somehow we need to find ways for the government to operate in Internet time when faced with bridging these gaps, and expedite approvals of funding to address them.

Turning my attention to Senate Bill 2037, the Science and Technology Emergency Mobilization Act, I believe this legislation can help by establishing a structure within the national Netguard framework to enable public and private sectors to work together more effectively when cyber events threaten our country's electronic infrastructure. This act intends to create an organized process and control structure to allow the private sector to provide the appropriate assistance in times of need, as well as a mechanism for the government to quickly locate and request assistance from qualified individuals within the private sector. These capabilities are useful to enable the country to react quickly and appropriately to cyber security issues, particularly when they impact our national infrastructure.

While I am supportive of the concept reflected in Senate bill 2037, I urge the Committee to think and act carefully in defining who and how the Netguard members are qualified and enlisted. We must be certain that the mechanism created to assist does not introduce new vulnerabilities, competitions or confusion. The urgency to get this infrastructure in place must be tempered with the need to get it right.

Within the great State of Oregon, industry and government are working together to create a consortium called Oregon RAINS, which stands for the Regional Alliance for Information and Network Security. I believe this effort could serve as a model for other states to organize their cyber resources. Oregon RAINS will be hosting Richard Clarke and other officials for a review of this important program in Oregon in early June.

In summary, I am in strong support of both these important acts as they enhance the underpinnings required to address many of these obstacles and challenges. They will enable us to work together more effectively to improve our cyber security capabilities, as well as to ensure we continue to advance the state-of-the-art development of our cyber capability.

Thank you, Mr. Chairman, and I would welcome any questions.

[The prepared statement of Mr. Starnes follows:]

PREPARED STATEMENT OF W. WYATT STARNES, PRESIDENT AND CHIEF EXECUTIVE OFFICER, TRIPWIRE, INC.

Good afternoon Mr. Chairman and Members of the Committee. My name is Wyatt Starnes, a founder, CEO and president of Tripwire, Inc. I have followed with great interest the activities of the federal government at this very critical time in our nation's history. I would like to commend this Subcommittee, led by Senator Wyden and Senator Allen, and their staff, in directing focus on the critical issues of Cyber-risk and Cyber-security.

I appreciate the opportunity to present before this Committee today.

For the past decade, the technology that is Tripwire has focused on data integrity assurance as a means to achieve higher levels of security, control, availability, and reliability of computing systems. Our focus has been on protecting critical computing infrastructure within the commercial and government sectors. Tripwire software has been deployed on hundreds of thousands of systems worldwide, including many inside of this building.

At Tripwire, we understand the importance of being able to rapidly detect, assess, and appropriately respond to threats, risks and even accidental changes to critical systems. Intrusions, computer viruses, logic bombs, hackers, "worm" programs, and badly written software can all lead to compromise, alteration and destruction of crucial information. Assuring the integrity and control of the ever-expanding digital infrastructure is crucial to our nation's financial viability as well as its safety and security. We understand that to fully manage the risks associated with maintaining information resources requires exerting positive control: our products enable that level of control.

It is as an information security professional and business leader—as well as a citizen—that I am here before you today to discuss the security and control of our nation's cyber-infrastructure, and why I have concluded that both Senate bill 2182, the "Cyber Security Research and Development Act" and Senate bill 2037, the "Science and Technology Emergency Mobilization Act" represent positive steps forward to safeguard our nation's somewhat fragile digital infrastructure.

Relative to Senate bill 2182, our company understands the importance of supporting and funding research within the university system. After all, our core technology was initially developed at Purdue University almost ten years ago under the direction of Professor Eugene Spafford. We later obtained the commercial rights to the technology and have built upon the Purdue work to create high-quality, commercial data integrity assurance solutions that are in wide use around the world, including prominent usage within most branches of the U.S. Government. Other fundamental information security technology, including security scanners, firewalls, VPNs, and intrusion detection systems all have roots in academic research at Purdue and elsewhere.

It is important to note that a considerable amount of this technology was developed without federal support, and often without any external support at all. Research efforts over the last decade conducted at leading universities such as Purdue have been supported almost entirely by small corporate contributions. Unfortunately, there has been no federal support for the kind of long-term and center-based research that is being conducted. We can only speculate at the solutions we might have in hand for today's problems had these researchers been supported at a more appropriate level.

Because of market pressures, including the recent economic downturn, industry support for leading academic programs with long-term vision has suffered. This scarcity of dollars has reduced the capacity of most academic programs, and may even threaten the existence of a few at a time when we are beginning to realize their importance. The small quantity of funds available, and their dominance by industry, tends to cause researchers to focus on "quick fix" patches instead of more fundamental solutions to society's cyber-weaknesses.

Consider:

- There are too few students studying cyber-security needs and issues;
- Too little is being spent to drive the technological research required to fight a war on the cyber-battle ground;
- There are too few researchers advancing the state of technology within the university system.
- There are not enough trained professors to develop and teach the courses to train a new generation of information security professionals.

Unless something significant changes, these problems may continue or worsen despite the best efforts of those of us working in cyber-security.

It is also necessary to provide mechanisms to allow public universities to accept equity from private industry in order to effectively capitalize on technology developed with public funding. Some states, including Oregon, currently limit or prohibit these transactions. Oregon is moving aggressively to remove these restrictions with a ballot initiative to change the states constitution. This effort has been largely driven by the private sector. We urge other states to begin the important processes to reverse restrictive provisions relating to technology transfer by and between public Universities and the private sector.

We support Senate bill 2182 as it provides a means to address these issues by creating and funding programs to stimulate new cyber-research and development. This should help to "prime the pump" enhancing our ability as a nation to stay ahead in the development of critical cyber-protection technologies.

There is no doubt that leading firms such as Tripwire will respond to immediate security needs by government and society at large. But we also believe it is vital that government take a role in ensuring that the creative minds in leading universities such as Purdue have the resources to work on the solutions we will need a decades from now, too.

Does this solve all our problems? No. The problem extends beyond university funding. We must enhance the coordination among state and federal government, the academic community, and private industry.

From my perspective as the CEO of a commercial company, we routinely see the desire and need for government and commercial entities to enhance their security processes. In many cases, especially within the government sector, the requirements to 'upgrade' critical systems come months or even years before the funding becomes available. It is in these critical gaps that our cyber-vulnerability as a nation is the greatest.

I urge the Congress to be aware of these gaps. Somehow, we need to find ways for government to operate in "Internet Time" when faced with bridging these gaps and expedite approvals and funding to address them.

Another area I would like to comment on are the issues of National and local coordination and cooperation. During the aftermath of the events of September 11, we've all heard stories of companies and organizations with the desire and expertise to help government agencies. However, they found there were limited cross-agency mechanisms to coordinate this interest and well-intended response.

I am convinced we should learn from these experiences as the same sorts of challenges exist when dealing with threats and incidents of a "cyber" nature.

This leads me to offer my comments on Senate bill 2037, the "Science and Technology Emergency Mobilization Act". I believe that this legislation can help by establishing a structure within the "National NetGuard" framework to enable the public and private sectors to work together more effectively when cyber-events threaten our country's electronic infrastructure.

This act intends to create an organized process and control structure to allow private sector to provide the appropriate assistance in times of need, as well as a mechanism for the government to quickly locate and request assistance from qualified individuals within the private sector.

These capabilities are useful to enable the country to react quickly and appropriately to cyber-security issues, particularly when they impact our national infrastructure.

While I am supportive of the concept reflected in Senate bill 2037 I urge the Committee to think and act carefully in defining who and how the NetGuard members are qualified and enlisted. We must be certain that the mechanism created to assist does not introduce new vulnerabilities, competitions, or confusion. The urgency to get this infrastructure in place must be tempered by the need to 'get it right'.

Within our great state of Oregon the Private Sector is marshaling its resources to address these gaps at a local level. The Oregon Regional Alliance for Information and Network Security, or RAINS, is a consortium of private and public sector organizations and individuals forming around the following mission:

- To contribute to U.S. defense and Homeland Security by providing solutions to critical cyber-security problems, and
- To expand Oregon's cyber-security cluster, creating jobs, cultivating technical innovation and education, and improving the state's economy.

I believe that this model can be extended nationally and dovetail with the initiatives proposed in Senate bill 2037. The Oregon RAINS project will be hosting Richard Clarke and other federal officials in Oregon to present this project on June 5–6, 2002.

Comments on Homeland Security

What the Committee is addressing today could be included under the rubric 'Homeland Security'. I think it important to remember that many of the weaknesses in our infrastructures that we are concerned about today were identified by experts in academia, industry and government decades ago. Those warnings were not heeded because they involved additional appropriations and regulation that were not seen as having an immediate effect. Thus, we are now faced with an urgent need and much larger economic and social cost to retrofit solutions—including some of dubious effectiveness—into everything from communication to transportation to power distribution.

Experts have likewise been warning for years that our information infrastructure is at risk and that insufficient investment is being made in research, education, and deployment of safeguards. I believe that proactively allocating and expediting significant funding to enhance our National digital infrastructure before there is a major breach would be very prudent.

Summary

In summary, I am in strong support of this important legislation as it enhances the underpinnings required to address many of these obstacles and challenges. It will enable us to work together more effectively to improve our cyber-security capabilities, as well as ensure that we continue to advance the state-of-the-art with regard to protecting our cyber-infrastructure.

Thank you and I welcome any questions from the Committee.

Senator WYDEN. Wyatt, thank you. That is very helpful. I commend you for all of the innovative work you all have done, and of course, Oregon RAINS really is a pioneering effort. As you know, we have worked very closely with them in our efforts to try to move the legislation we are considering today. We are glad you are here. We will have some questions.

Mr. Hira, welcome.

STATEMENT OF RONIL HIRA, INSTITUTE OF ELECTRICAL AND ELECTRONICS ENGINEERS (EEE)–USA

Mr. HIRA. Thank you, Mr. Chairman. Good afternoon. I wanted to thank you, the Ranking Member, and distinguished Subcommittee Members for inviting me here today. My name is Ronil Hira, and I am here on behalf of the 235,000 U.S. members of the Institute of Electrical and Electronics Engineers.

I am the chair of the IEEE–USA, which is our acronym here, the IEEE–USA's Research and Development Policy Committee. Our members are electrical, electronics, computer and software engineers who work in government, industry, as private consultants, as well as professors and students in universities.

We at IEEE–USA applaud the Subcommittee's efforts to address shortfalls in two critical areas related to homeland security today, disaster response and mobilization, and cyber security research and development. I think it is pretty axiomatic that technology is driving society, but it is also becoming pervasive within society in making things more and more complex. At the same time, we have an increase in terms of the threats and vulnerabilities to outside threats.

Fortunately, the United States has the largest and best-qualified pool of technological experts and the most sophisticated technology and communications equipment in the world. The challenge, however, is in coordinating the response, finding the necessary experts and supplies, and getting them into play as quickly as possible. For this reason, IEEE–USA strongly endorses the objectives of S. 2037, the Science and Technology Emergency Mobilization Act.

Technology evaluation and standards are important elements in any implementation, but they are really critical elements in any disaster recovery program, and I am glad to see that is being addressed here. In addition, interoperability is obviously critical in those disaster recovery programs. I do not think you have to be an American politics scholar of Alexis de Tocqueville to know and recognize the degree to which volunteerism and voluntary organizations are important in the U.S., so I am glad that S. 2037 does address that.

In regard to S. 2182, the Cyber Security Research and Development Act, we were supporters of the legislation when it was introduced the House, H.R. 3394. A couple of points on that. It is not the case that cyber security and computer security has not been going on. Really, the issue is the scale in which it has been going on. There are clients such as military, financial services, who are very concerned about it and have addressed computer security to whatever degrees.

The real issue becomes, to what degree is computer security impacting all of technology development, software development, and so on and so forth, and we believe that this bill will help to address that.

The point is not just to advance the state-of-the-art, but is to advance the state of the market and the state of the practice that is out there, and we believe S. 2182 is comprehensive enough to get us in the right direction moving toward that. It includes industry, government, and universities working together. You are going to get incremental gains, but you are also going to push the frontiers of cyber security. For those reasons, we are pleased to support S. 2182, and I look forward to any questions you might have.

[The prepared statement of Mr. Hira follows:]

PREPARED STATEMENT OF RONIL HIRA, INSTITUTE OF ELECTRICAL AND ELECTRONICS ENGINEERS (EEE)–USA

I would like to thank the Chairman, Ranking Member and distinguished Subcommittee Members for inviting me here today. My name is Ronil Hira, I am here on behalf of the more than 235,000 U.S. members of The Institute of Electrical and Electronics Engineers. I am the chair of IEEE–USA's Research and Development Policy Committee. Our members are electrical, electronics, computer and software engineers who work in government and industry, as private consultants and are professors and students in our universities.

We at IEEE–USA applaud the Subcommittee's efforts to address shortfalls in two critical areas related to homeland security: disaster response and mobilization, and cyber security research and development. As the nation becomes more dependent upon technology in nearly every aspect of our lives, the level of vulnerability to technological disruption rises accordingly, as does the potential impact that disruption has on our lives. As we saw with the problems that became apparent following the attacks of September 11, the promptness and quality of the technological response to terrorist attacks or natural disasters could mean the difference between life and death.

Fortunately, the United States has the largest and best-qualified pool of technological experts and the most sophisticated technology and communications equipment in the world. The challenge, however, is in coordinating the response, finding the necessary experts and supplies and getting them into place as quickly as possible.

For this reason, IEEE–USA strongly endorses the objectives of the S. 2037, the Science and Technology Mobilization Act. The concept of organizing to focus the nation's technology resources to address the response to terrorist attacks and other emergencies is an important ingredient in a robust homeland defense. As a result of the attacks, local governments are renewing their efforts to design disaster-recovery plans. Many entities have put in place emergency communication plans and have taken steps to ensure optimal use of other technologies. For example, uninterruptible power supplies are now coming into common usage.

We strongly concur with Office of Science and Technology Policy Director, Dr. John Marburger's recommendation encouraging voluntary preparedness among organizations, including implementing IT disaster-recovery procedures as well as promoting standards for coordinating disaster-recovery responses. This may well fit into the charter of the National Institute of Standards and Technology; however, IEEE–USA does not take a position on which governmental agency should be charged with overseeing the overall program envisioned by the legislation We do feel that NIST, if designated, and industry can work within the framework of a center for civilian homeland security technology evaluation as envisioned by the legislation to develop standards and protocols to serve as models for local disaster-recovery programs. The standards can not only enable optimal use of technology within a local environment, but can allow for sharing of resources to respond to a regional disaster.

The infrastructure reliability advisory board as described in the legislation can work with the center to define best practices on how to make technology and communications infrastructure less vulnerable. This will enable the board to make recommendations on all aspects of deployment of emergency response and recovery of technological and communications systems.

We urge caution in proceeding to establish the National Emergency Technology Response Teams. It is important to recognize that communication and other technological systems can be extremely complicated, requiring not only general knowledge of the technical factors but also specific knowledge of the system under stress. This may only be available in the company and its vendors that installed the system originally. Furthermore, if a local government has a sound disaster-recovery program, it may not be feasible, and could be counter-productive, to attempt to bring in teams that have not been integrated into the established program.

One valuable service that the U.S. government can perform is to evaluate and critique local disaster-recovery programs. This could consist of plan review and test observation. The government has many agencies with expertise in this kind of service.

In regard to S. 2182, the Cyber Security Research and Development Act, IEEE–USA has been a strong supporter of this legislation since the companion bill was introduced in the House of Representatives. There are many excellent provisions in this bill. I would like to highlight one in particular. The Chairman, and author of the legislation, has done a remarkable job in understanding the richness of our research enterprise and symbiotic relationships. Specifically, the bill includes research that will be conducted in universities, government and industry. Each of these institutions brings something important to the table when it comes to research.

In addition, the bill recognizes the importance of training future professionals. While some of these folks will become cyber security researchers and professors, many will become cyber security practitioners. The purpose of research is not only to advance the state of the art, but also to ultimately advance its application in the marketplace. Only through all of the mechanisms in this bill will we be able to achieve both. In order to advance the state of the art and the state of the market, we need to advance the state of the science in cyber security. Systematic research is the way in which the cyber security profession can codify its lessons learned, develop its common language, and most importantly, advance the practice of cyber security.

IEEE–USA is pleased to support S. 2182, which will pay dividends not only for protection against cyber terrorism, but also for commerce and personal privacy.

Thank you very much.

Senator WYDEN. Mr. Logan.

STATEMENT OF JEFFREY LOGAN, BUSINESS DEVELOPMENT MANAGER, M/A–COM, INC., WIRELESS SYSTEMS

Mr. LOGAN. Thank you, Chairman Wyden, Senator Allen, and other distinguished members of the Science, Technology, & Space Subcommittee. It is an honor to have this opportunity to appear before you today and assist your efforts in strengthening our nation's information infrastructure and improve our capability to respond and recover from terrorist attacks and other emergencies.

I am Jeffrey Logan, business development manager for M/A–COM Wireless, Incorporated. M/A–COM Wireless Systems is currently deploying fully interoperable statewide public safety radio systems in Pennsylvania and Florida. We have recently been selected to provide county communications systems in the Oakland County, Michigan, and city communications for San Antonio and Oklahoma City.

Our company is a world leader in the development and global manufacture of radio components and network solutions for the wireless telecommunications industry. I appreciate this opportunity comment on S. 2037, the Science and Technology Emergency Mobilization Act, regarding recommendations for ensuring that emergency officials and first responders have access to effective and reliable wireless communications capability, and the establishment of state pilot projects aimed at achieving interoperability for emergency preparedness.

One of the key concerns for first responders is interoperability. Lack of interoperability occurs when public safety personnel respond to the same emergency but cannot communicate with each other because they have an incompatible radio system, or they are on different frequencies. Lack of interoperability wastes time, wastes effort, and it can risk lives. Safety of life and property can only be assured when public safety agencies can easily communicate with each other. All too often the different systems they use would preclude them from communicating at all.

Agencies must have high-quality communications at their disposal to ensure effective and timely coordination during a disaster. Recent high profile incidents, coupled with the events of September 11, have drawn into sharp focus the need for voice radio interoperability. Interoperability is both a technology and management challenge. S. 2037 should include consideration of training, organization, coverage, funding, frequency availability, and incident coordination.

It is our recommendation that state pilot projects should include both technical and nontechnical considerations, as well as new approaches to policy in the development of interoperable solutions. A number of states have already made significant headway toward interoperability. The establishment of state pilot programs should build on many of the innovative communication technology advances already achieved in states such as Pennsylvania, Maryland, and Florida.

What is the best way to achieve interoperability for our nation's first responders? One solution would be to require state and local government to replace today's fully functioning radios and infrastructure with new equipment that would be based on a single standard. FEMA has estimated the cost to pursue this course to replace all our nation's public safety radios to be in excess of $40 billion. Creating a single radio system standard does not necessarily solve interoperability. Several operational issues, including sufficient communications spectrum and channel management, would still be needed to be resolved.

We do agree, Dr. Hoffman, however, that standards should be encouraged, particularly in the area of networking standards, such as established Ethernet and TCIP protocols. An alternate approach, we feel the best approach to our interoperability is to connect existing systems into regional, statewide, and national systems which would provide multiagency interoperability without requiring different agencies to purchase new radio equipment. This could be done for a fraction of the cost.

Interconnecting or networking existing systems is the quickest and most cost-effective way to deploy. This is because the network supports all existing radio infrastructure, allowing agencies to use radios, repeaters, and frequencies already in place. We think this makes sense in order to optimize the President's $1.3 billion first responder interoperability budget, leveraging this money to as many communities as possible.

A good example of pioneering interoperability is underway right now in a statewide system in Pennsylvania. In 1995, Governor Tom Ridge and Lieutenant Governor Mark Schweiker came into office. They inherited an antiquated radio system. The existing network was more than 20 years old, and becoming impossible to maintain. In fact, it really was a patchwork of several incompatible systems. As a result, Governor Ridge has replaced this with a fully interoperability statewide communications system.

In conclusion, I would like to commend to the Members of the Subcommittee for their legislative efforts to enhance the security of the nation's infrastructure and our ability to respond to national emergencies. Lack of communications interoperability is not a new condition. We have two ways to address interoperability. One solution would be to replace today's fully functional radios and infrastructure with a cost-prohibitive solution. A second and alternate approach would be to connect existing systems in a way that we could leverage fully functional systems to our benefit.

Thank you for the opportunity to appear before you today. I would be pleased to answer any questions you may have.

[The prepared statement of Mr. Logan follows:]

PREPARED STATEMENT OF JEFFREY LOGAN, BUSINESS DEVELOPMENT MANAGER, M/A–COM, INC., WIRELESS SYSTEMS

Thank you, Chairman Wyden, Senator Allen, and other distinguished Members of the Science, Technology, and Space Subcommittee. It is an honor to have this opportunity to appear before you today and to assist in your efforts to strengthen our nation's information infrastructure and improve our capability to respond and recover from terrorist attacks and other emergencies.

I am Jeffrey M. Logan, Business Development Manager for M/A–COM Wireless Systems Inc. M/A–COM Wireless Systems is currently deploying fully interoperable statewide public safety radio systems in Pennsylvania and Florida. We have also recently been selected to provide county communications systems for Oakland County Michigan, and city communications for San Antonio and Oklahoma City. Our company is a world leader in the development and global manufacture of radio components and network solutions for the wireless telecommunications industry. Additionally, M/A–COM Wireless Systems is supported as a wholly owned unit of Tyco International, the world's largest manufacturer and servicer of electrical and electronic components.

I appreciate this opportunity to comment on S. 2037, the Science and Technology Emergency Mobilization Act, regarding recommendations for ensuring that emergency officials and first responders have access to effective and reliable wireless communications capabilities and the establishment of state pilot projects aimed at achieving interoperability for emergency preparedness agencies.

The Pursuit of Interoperability

One of the key concerns for the first responders (police, fire, EMS) is interoperability. Lack of interoperability occurs when public safety personnel respond to the same emergency but cannot communicate with each other because they operate on incompatible radio systems or on different frequency bands. Lack of interoperability wastes time, wastes effort, and can risk lives. Safety of life and property can only be assured when public safety agencies can easily communicate with one another. All too often, the different systems they use preclude them from communicating at all. Agencies must have high-quality, interoperable communications at their disposal to ensure effective and timely coordination of disaster responses. Recent high-profile incidents, coupled with the events of September 11, have drawn into sharp focus the need for voice radio interoperability both for routine day-to-day use and during emergencies.

"So poor were communications that on one side of the trade center complex, in the city's emergency management headquarters, a city engineer warned officials that the towers were at risk of "near imminent collapse," but those he told could not reach the highest-ranking fire chief by radio. Instead, a messenger was sent across acres, dodging flaming debris and falling bodies, to deliver this assessment in person. He arrived with the news less than a minute before the first tower fell." [1]

Achieving Interoperability

Interoperability is both a technology and a management challenge. Consideration should include training, organization, coverage, funding, frequency availability and incident coordination. It is our recommendations that state pilot projects should include both technical and non-technical considerations, as well as new approaches to policy, in the development of interoperability solutions. A number of states have already made significant headway toward interoperability. The establishment of state pilot programs should build on many of the innovative communication technology advances already achieved in states such as Pennsylvania, Maryland and Florida.

What is the best way to achieve interoperability for our nations First Responders?

One solution would be to require state and local governments to replace today's fully functional radios and infrastructure with new equipment that would be based on a single radio system standard. FEMA has estimated the cost to pursue this course to replace all our nation's public safety radio systems to be in excess of $40 billion. Creating a single radio system standard does not necessarily solve interoperability. Several operational issues including sufficient communications spectrum and channel management would still be needed to be resolved. However, networking standards such as established Ethernet and TCIP protocols should be leveraged to enable network-to-network communications and voice over IP applications. An alternate approach to interoperability is to interconnect existing systems into regional, statewide or national systems, which would provide multi-agency interoperability without requiring different agencies to purchase new radio equipment—for a fraction of the cost to replace all in-service radio systems. Interconnecting or networking existing systems is the quickest and most cost effective to deploy. This is because the network supports all existing radio infrastructure, allowing agencies to use radios, repeaters and frequency allocations that are already in place. We think this makes sense in order to optimize the President's proposed $1.3 billion first responder interoperability budget to as many communities as possible.

Best Practices

A good example of pioneering interoperability is underway right now on a statewide system in Pennsylvania. Back in 1995, when Governor Tom Ridge and Lt. Governor Mark Schweiker came to office, they inherited an antiquated radio system. The existing radio network was more than 20 years old and was becoming impossible to maintain. In fact, it really was a patchwork of several incompatible networks serving 23 state agencies. Former Governor Ridge recognized that the out-

[1] Jim Dwyer and Kevin Flynn "Before the Towers Fell, Fire Dept. Fought Chaos" *The New York Times,* January 30, 2002, pp. 1.

moded, stand-alone radio systems limited communications between state agencies and local government, particularly during emergencies. It also squandered opportunities for cost savings through shared equipment purchases and mutual aid agreements.

As a result, in 1996, Governor Ridge launched a multi-year project to modernize and unify state agencies' two-way radio systems. M/A–COM was selected to provide the radio equipment for the project utilizing IP network technology.

This year, when the new system is fully deployed, it will tie Commonwealth agencies and participating local governments into a single, more reliable, high-capacity radio network. A key advantage of the new radio network is that state and local government will be able to communicate with each other through voice over IP networking technology. Additionally, system elements, such as radio towers and transmitters, will be shared across state agencies, thereby holding down costs. Most importantly, the new system will greatly enhance first responders' ability to respond to emergencies quickly and in a coordinated manner. In fact, Pennsylvania's new radio network, completed under Governor Mark Schweiker, will be the first truly interoperable statewide voice and data public safety radio system in the entire country.

Conclusion

In summary, I commend the Members of the Subcommittee for their legislative efforts to enhance the security of our nation's infrastructure and our ability to respond to national emergencies. Lack of communications interoperability is not a new condition. We have two ways to address lack of interoperability. One solution would be to replace today's fully functional radios and infrastructure with new equipment at a prohibitive cost and years of deployment. An alternate approach is to connect existing systems together using voice over IP networking technology, immediately and affordably. M/A–COM Wireless Systems, Inc. stands ready to support government research and development in this area.

Thank you for the opportunity to appear before you today. I would be pleased to answer any questions you might have.

Senator WYDEN. Thank you, Mr. Logan. Let me start with you, if I could, Dr. Strawn. Some of the information security experts today are painting a bleak picture. They paint a dire picture of the current state of the discipline. They say there are only about 100 professors. There are only a few centers. There are only a handful of Ph.D's in information sciences, and suffice it to say, this is what the Congress is seeking to address.

Now, you discuss the need for more researchers in the area of course in your testimony. S. 2182 addresses the problem by increasing the investments in research and training generally. This relates to information security. In your view, how long would it take, with this legislation, to start seeing some tangible improvements in these numbers?

Dr. STRAWN. I think several years would show some pretty good progress. We have the experience of this first year of our Trusted Computer program, small as it is, which did show that the professoriate in computer science responded to turn its attention increasingly to this area, and so I think additional support and focus can be a very valuable way of building up the size of the professoriate and the size of the student body that will attack these problems.

Senator WYDEN. And how long do you think it will take before our country sees tangible improvements in the research that is undertaken in the information security field? There are two things we have to do here. We have to deal with the shortage of professors, and we have to beef up the research that is undertaken in the field. Tell me about tangible improvements.

Dr. STRAWN. I think there are opportunities both for short-term research benefits and for the long-term research benefits. As the words express, of course, it will take longer for the long-term understanding to filter into technologies and services that I think will ultimately provide the best solutions, but I think we have observed that already there are developments in the private sector and by the professoriate some very good steps, intermediate steps, let us say, to improve our security; and solutions range all the way from broader education to train new work force members to putting into place services and security products and processes that we already know about but have not had as much success getting into broad use as we would like.

In a certain sense, that requires a certain amount of social science research as well to understand better how we can put what we know into practice more quickly.

Senator WYDEN. Tell me what you believe to be the most important areas that warrant further research and examination, and why. Take two or three, for example, of the areas that you think are the most important from the standpoint of research and information security, tell me what those areas are, and why.

Dr. STRAWN. I will do that with the caveat that NSF's approach usually is to ask the research professors who we work with what are the most promising areas they find, and then when their peers are able to look at those proposals and tell us that these are the really promising areas, then we feel very comfortable that, having the smartest friends in the world, we know what we are talking about.

Some of the things we have already been told and that I certainly agree with is the importance of looking at the whole picture. As I said before, secure components do not a secure system make; and science has very frequently progressed in great ways by dividing and conquering, looking at small portions of a subject and knowing more and more about it.

Security is really a different sort of a beast, in that we must keep a system focus. We must develop the science of the whole system in order to make sure that secure systems will result from secure components, and so I think that is probably one of the most important technical areas.

I think a second is the interdisciplinary problem of finding how we can more rapidly introduce advances once we have made them: enabling our organizations to accept beneficial changes more rapidly. We have been working with our social scientists quite a bit in the last several years looking at these types of interdisciplinary problems. I think in the short term that could be a very valuable step.

Senator WYDEN. Any other areas?

Dr. STRAWN. Those are the first two that come to mind.

Senator WYDEN. Dr. Hoffman, do you want to try that one, too? What are the most important areas, in your view, for information security research? Give me, if you would, two or three, and tell me why you think that is the case.

Dr. HOFFMAN. Well, you are asking a tough question when you say limit it to two or three, but I will attempt to limit it to two or three.

I would agree that absolutely the most important is to have a big picture, and to look at interdisciplinary research, because when you are dealing with computer security you are tying together disciplines of computer science, electrical engineering, management, forensics, law, and various practices, and all sorts of other things, so it is not only a technological solution. Computer security involves a lot of areas, and they are not only technological, so the interdisciplinary part, including public acceptance, including market acceptance, is very important, so that is one, okay.

You said two or three. I will give you two others. Architecture. I think we have been using the same computer architecture effectively linked together in networks, for about 50 or 60 years. There may be other architectures that could be looked at that could help protect—separate data from programs in a way that would very much enhance security, so computer architecture is another area.

Finally, as I mentioned in my testimony, wireless. In the not-too-distant future we are going to have very many more wireless devices than we do now, and, as usual, utility is going to trump security the way we are going now. Unfortunately, this is going to lead to some security problems, unless we really get a handle on the existing wireless situation and deal with it whether it is in the wireless devices or in network protocols, or whatever.

Senator WYDEN. So what do you think the wireless issues are?

Dr. HOFFMAN. What do I think the wireless issues are? There are a bunch of them. For one thing, the existing protocols have been shown to be not sufficient for security. In addition, when they are connected together you have all sorts of applications that are going to be developed using wireless. Take one example, intelligent vehicle systems. If people are driving along or being transported along in squadrons of intelligent vehicles, and the vehicles are communicating with each other, they have to be authenticated, authorized, and at the same time there are privacy issues involved as well. That is just one example.

Senator WYDEN. Let us return, then, to you Dr. Strawn, and compare, if you would, the cyber security program that you have now against S. 2182. The program that you have now, research includes a scholarship for service program that provides scholarships to undergraduates and graduate students that study computer security. Then they have to serve the federal government, obviously, for a couple of years. What do you see as the big differences between your current program, the scholarship for service program, and what is envisaged in the Senate and House bills?

Dr. STRAWN. I would say that what we are doing now has some great similarities to what is proposed in the bills, and the major difference is scope and size. The work that we are doing, as I mentioned in my testimony, is on the order of $10 million a year investment, and I observe that the bills propose roughly an order of magnitude increase.

Senator WYDEN. Tell me what you think the lessons are with respect to what science and technology can do in emergency response and homeland security after September 11. I mean, my sense, and what has really drawn me into this cause, is that there is a chance to mobilize a generation, a generation that was raised on digital technologies that wants to contribute, wants to help. We have been struck by how many companies and individuals are willing to come forward and say, as long as the government does not waste my time, I am going to pitch-in.

People from Intel, for example, do not want to spend a lot of time standing around, and unfortunately, in the effort to respond on September 11, some of those private sector efforts were wasted. So, one of the lessons I have learned from September 11 is that I think there is a chance to mobilize a huge number of people with expertise in IT and expertise in various scientific areas, and harness that energy and talent and bring it to bear. But, I would like to have you tell me what you think the lessons with respect to the role of government can play now in science and technology policy to both prevent and respond to the kinds of problems we faced on September 11.

Dr. STRAWN. First of all, I agree with everything you have said in terms of some lessons to be taken away from it, that we have had a terrible wake-up call, and it focused the energies of the nation in a way that we now must turn to positive results.

One of the areas, as I mentioned previously, that we are concerned about is that not enough faculty have been specializing in security research. I think this situation has produced in students and faculty alike more of a focus on the importance of cyber security, and if we can respond properly to that increased interest, it will be much to our benefit to do so.

I would also mention in support of Professor Hoffman's comment about computer architecture, and as mentioned in my written testimony, computer security was an add-on to the original design of information processing systems. We weren't thinking as much about that in the early fifties as we are now, 50 years later, and many of our researchers have suggested that a great, fundamental research opportunity would be to go back and rethink the fundamental design of information processing systems with security as a design criterion and requirement, rather than a later add-on to be patched on the side.

Senator WYDEN. That is what you would call a big lesson. That will be a big exercise, but I think you are right. I think that is really something that the government ought to be researching, and I think that is a thoughtful answer. Why do we not just go down the panel at this point, and I would be interested—we can start with you, Dr. Hoffman, then go to Wyatt, but tell us, if you would, what you think the experience of September 11 says in terms of lessons for science and technology policy as we try to both respond and prevent these terrorism problems.

Dr. HOFFMAN. Well, one thing it indicated to me was the importance of thinking ahead, and the importance of then acting on the lessons. To give you one example, we routinely teach exercises, and the George Washington University has about seven courses in the Computer Science Department, and another seven or eight in the Engineering Management and Systems Engineering department dealing with computer security information assurance, and related topics.

Many of these courses deal with vulnerability assessment, and we do scenarios. We actually run—one of my favorites is one developed by the Rand Corporation called The Day After, where you basically sit up a situation, say, 2 years hence, in 2004. You say, here is the situation on the ground. One bad thing happens, another bad thing happens, and you expose students to this, and in essence they cannot deal with it. It is sort of a classic in-box exercise, although worse, and then they go back to 2002, to today, and say, okay, what should we do now, and that is in essence what you are doing.

I think the most important thing learned is, if we had been able to more put into effect those actions which we had dealt with in the classroom in real life on September 11, then September 12 we would have been much better off, so just getting people to think that way is the first step, and then getting action plans developed is the next one.

Senator WYDEN. Mr. Starnes.

Mr. STARNES. Yes, Mr. Chairman. I think there are a number of issues that came as a result of learning from September 11. Speaking to the positive side of technology for a moment, there were many systems, Internet systems, wireless systems that were still operable and played a very important role throughout the unfolding of September 11, even with that as a factor.

Senator WYDEN. I think it is striking none of the satellite systems had problems. All of the satellite systems worked.

Mr. STARNES. And a fair amount of interconnect was still in place, and for a while the only communication some people had was via the electronic non-analog infrastructure, which I think is striking. There were also major vulnerability points, major hubs of connectivity that even though we thought they were redundant hubs, we did not plan for the magnitude of the damage that was done.

But speaking to the broader issue of the short-term issues, long-term issues, I am coming at this from a commercial angle, which is a slightly different angle than my colleagues on the academic side. The way we see spending in cyber security, it is sort of the spray paint, the moving car problem. In other words, we are trying to get to a destination, and we are trying to get their fast, but we have got to get paint on the car along the way. In other words, we have to protect ourselves while we are getting there, so we really need to divide our thinking into two areas.

We have some short-term issues we need to deal with, and there are evolving technologies in the form of data integrity assurance and intrusion detection and other technologies that play a valuable role. At the same time, we need to develop a longer-term view of how technology should be constructed in a world where we have the bigger security issues now than we anticipated when the original designs were done, as Dr. Strawn said, many years ago.

So I think we have to move in parallel. We have to give money to government, to commercial industry to protect themselves now. At the same time, we feed money to universities to begin to reverse the course of the attrition we have seen in the cyber research and cyber security arena, and I think both of those paths have to be moved on in parallel.

Senator WYDEN. Mr. Hira.

Mr. HIRA. Mr. Chairman, I think the major thing that came to my mind was really the vulnerability, but also the human dimensions that are involved in technology and how dependent that we have, really the average person has become on technology, and the fact that we open the cell phone and we expect it to work, and so I really think that the major lesson there was that the systems were not designed for this kind of event in mind, and we have to rethink the way we design these products so that we accommodate new criteria. It has really changed the criteria to which we have to design these products.

Senator WYDEN. Mr. Logan.

Mr. LOGAN. Mr. Chairman, I believe—three major areas of lessons learned with regard to wireless. We are also a private company, and certainly recognize the President's budget that is being proposed for first responders, as many private companies do, but we also recognize there is a lot of competition for that money, and we have to be very smart in how we apply those funds to curing the problems.

With regard to interoperability, we could certainly apply money in a way that would maybe have new equipment, but the equipment in the end still could not talk to each other. We need to consider how we can interconnect our existing infrastructures in a way that people can communicate. We have to look very hard at training and invest in training, because when these events happen, as all the first responders' reports have said, training, and preparation upfront, the technology alone will not provide the answer. It has to work in concert with the technology.

I guess the third item would be where we have various first responders showing up to an event, trying to communicate with each other, not having the ability to have coverage, so I think as we look at this bill, as we can apply moneys to providing mobile coverage, bringing communication to the site and the scene of an incident would go a long way in solving future problems.

Senator WYDEN. Very good points, and we are struck by what both you and Mr. Hira have talked about, the human dimension of all of this. I think our hearing where we heard from the head of the fire fighting effort at the Pentagon, and we had people hand-carrying messages in to firemen, little snippets of paper, hand-carrying them in. I am glad you two brought it back to people, because it is important, and wireless can make a real difference in that area.

Let me, if I might, turn to this question of how we are going to mobilize the volunteers, and Dr. Strawn, you are welcome to participate in this as well. You have heard me comment on this, that the Administration is being very helpful in terms of working with us. It has not fully developed a position, but you are welcome nonetheless to offer your ideas and thoughts here on the strategic technology reserve. I will initially direct this to Dr. Hoffman and Mr. Starnes.

What we want to do is say, "Look, in this country we have got a strategic petroleum reserve, so that when there is a crunch with respect to energy, we are in a position to address that." What I envisage is something along the lines of a strategic technology reserve, so all across this country, when faced with bioterrorism efforts or other sorts of dire kinds of threats and problems, it is possible to mobilize people and equipment fairly readily, and some of this does not strike me as particularly hard and cumbersome to do.

For example, we were struck how in most communities, for example, there is not even a list of people who would have some expertise in these various health agencies. Say that a community, say Portland, or another community, was hit by a bioterrorism agent. It ought to be possible to fairly quickly turn to a list of medical experts and others that you could call on for help. What we would like to do is develop that kind of data base of volunteers and experts, and virtually everyone we have talked to in terms of municipalities, first responders and others, said absolutely we think it would be very useful to have that on hand, and this would involve a pretty modest role for government.

This is essentially making sure that you have this group available when you face these kinds of calamities. I think the points that you are making with respect to authentication and security mechanisms and making sure the data base is not misused or, as you said, Mr. Starnes, taken over by people with malevolent intentions—I want to make it clear, I think that is significant.

I think it is important, but I assume, just so we are clear for the record, you two do not think those kinds of issues are insurmountable. What you think is they are issues that Congress has got to get right. Congress has got to work with the private sector in order to get them right, but you certainly do not see this as creating some kind of insurmountable burden that would keep us from having a data base of technology and expertise and equipment around the country, do you?

Mr. STARNES. Mr. Chairman, I will take that first. Absolutely not. One of the things we definitely were struck with post 9/11 is the amazing spirit and patriotism of the American people, as well as their just creativity and drive, and really that is the response that motivated both private and local government sectors within our State of Oregon to get together and see if we could organize better and prepare better in advance, and it was striking to us on the organizing Committee how poorly prepared we really are in terms of, as you point out, even knowing who to go to in the case of a potential cyber terrorism issue, and what the resources are.

So the first set of procedures we are going through is essentially inventorying our intellectual skills within the state, and the next part of that exercise will be determining how we catalyze those and how we interconnect those in a useful and effective fashion. Absolutely these problems can be taken care of over the long haul.

I do believe that private industry needs to be heavily involved in that process. We need to think about issues of data base redundancy and network vulnerabilities and so on to make sure that we plan and build the network that has to support the people involved in advance, and contemplating a number of the different threats that might be present.

Senator WYDEN. Dr. Hoffman.

Dr. HOFFMAN. Mr. Chairman, I agree with everything Mr. Starnes has said. I agree that it is not an insurmountable problem. I also want to point out that we will never solve the problem perfectly, but if we can get a solution that is 90 percent further along than where we are today, I think we would have made obviously great progress.

One thing that is important to realize—I take some of this from my experience serving in my local town where I reside, in Chevy Chase, Maryland, yet we had a committee for Y2K, which I served on, and just knowing the local resources and going up to the county level and so forth on up is very important.

So I think rather than having one grand system defined, this might be an excellent opportunity to have a number of local systems deployed, tried out, tried out in the laboratory of the states or even at a lower level of government, and keep the communication system flowing between all the levels of government and the private sector, that would be, I think, a better way to architect it than put all of your eggs in one basket.

Senator WYDEN. I think those are thoughtful points. We are going to work with you, because I think you are right. You cannot come up with any ideal kind of approach that ensures that you never have a bug anywhere at any time, but I really do see a strategic technology reserve as an insurance policy for this country. Given how many people have said they would help, major companies in this country have said, "Look, we will get people and equipment when the country's national security interest and well-being are affected by these terrorist attacks." It just seems a shame to not try to address some of these issues I advance and not just have all these well-meaning people basically in a position of heading to some disaster site and kind of standing around. That is what some have told us happened in New York, and it is not because New York did a crummy job. Quite the opposite. New York City did a terrific job. How they accomplished so much so quickly is an extraordinary success story.

What else could have been done is what I think we want to look at, and of course, most communities are not in a position to have the resources you had in New York City. We are going to work very closely with you to iron out these questions of authentication and privacy and making sure you do not have a system that gets hijacked by the very people you are trying to deal with in terms of the overall effort.

It was interesting you mentioned Y2K, Dr. Hoffman, because that was an area we wanted to look at, and maybe we can bring you back into this.

Dr. Strawn, I was very involved in the Y2K efforts that this Committee tackled under the leadership of Chairman Hollings and Senator McCain, and obviously, a lot of those paid off. That concerted effort to have people working together and preparing for a wide variety of potential threats to this country paid big dividends. I would be curious if this panel thinks there were any parallels to be drawn or any lessons between the Y2K effort and what we are doing now to try to improve cyber security.

Dr. STRAWN. I would be happy to take a crack at that. I had the good fortune of also being involved in the Y2K efforts at NSF. I had an interesting assignment. NSF undertook, as part of its public knowledge and public education of science tasks, to run a series of surveys, polls of the public to find out what their knowledge was and what their concerns were about the Y2K issue as it went forward; I had the good fortune of serving as NSF's spokesperson during that time on that subject.

We observed that, number one, as Y2K approached, it focused the attention and the efforts of the country very greatly toward solving the problem. Number two, the more information that was made available to the public and the more they understood what was going on, the less concern they had, and the more they understood what was happening, and that was a general, very good benefit of education.

If I may add one other subject relating to a government analog of the volunteerism that you were discussing a moment ago. I observed that since September 11, there has been a very vital and vigorous interaction between the defense community and the civilian research community, we are working together to make sure that research results that have been developed in universities and the civilian sector are available to the defense and security activities that need advanced research and development. That is not quite volunteerism, but it has the same very beneficial effects of propelling these advances forward.

Senator WYDEN. Other panel members, parallels between Y2K and what we are trying to do here?

Mr. STARNES. I think that is a very interesting and relevant question. One of the advantages of the Y2K issue is that we had a specific and imminent date to work toward, and in the few years ahead of Y2K—the industry estimates range a bit on this, but the upward estimates are that there was almost $300 billion spent on Y2K preparedness.

I think it is very interesting to sort of compare that with the industry spending for security technologies in the last 3 years, the composite industry spending, which has been about, somewhat under $20 billion, so on a single incident, that was a very known and measured incident as an industry, as a country we spent almost $300 billion, and cumulatively over the last 3 years we have spent about $20 billion, so I think that really points to a gap, still, in the way we need to look at funding these really important vulnerabilities that we have.

Senator WYDEN. Okay. Let's move back to the topic, if we could, of the strategic technology reserve. Mr. Hira, I would like to ask you a question, because, of course, your organization represents a large number of technology experts, and I think it would be helpful to get your sense of whether there would be a lot of those individuals and companies that would be willing to volunteer.

My sense is that they are looking for a chance to help and participate, and in a situation like this say, if there is a problem in my area, or a problem in my region of the country, we are anxious to be there. We will volunteer; we are sending our name and saying we want to participate in something like the strategic technology reserve. What is your sense about whether the people you work with would say if their expertise is needed emergency officials could know where to find them?

Mr. HIRA. I am glad you asked that question, actually, because we are a volunteer-driven organization. We do not have industrial membership. Our membership is as individuals. We are structured along a couple of different dimensions, but the two important dimensions that are relevant to this are, one, based on your technical expertise, or your subdiscipline. So, for example, my area is control systems. Somebody else's is antennas and propagation, and so on and so forth, and so there is a technology and technical dimension, but we are also organized geographically via regions and sections.

I do not see any reason why something like this could not or should not appeal to many of our members that are out there.

Senator WYDEN. Let me turn now to the part of our legislation that calls for setting up a clearinghouse or test bed, and maybe we can hear from Mr. Starnes and Mr. Logan, I think both would be good for this question.

What we are dealing with here is this: the federal government has received thousands and thousands of ideas and proposals to fund various technologies and products. In effect, it is a new deluge. Thousands of them have come from across the country, and what Senator Allen and I are trying to do is to make sure that we can perform a service for agencies, help them to identify new technologies, figure out if the proposed technologies can meet the specifications needed by the agencies.

We do not want new mandates, picking winners and losers and all of this sort of thing, but I think we can begin this round, Mr. Starnes and Mr. Logan, with whether you think the current emergency response agencies are doing enough to harness the potential of new technological developments, and whether we need to do a better job of trying to be open to new technologies so that we can use all of this talent.

Mr. STARNES. Mr. Chairman, I will take that one first.

Clearly, I think we can be doing a better job. I think there are some wonderful agencies, certainly in the area of security awareness. CERT has done an admirable job for the amount of funding and support that they have received, but we are dealing with a really big issue here, and we really have not, as a nation, been under a coordinated attack. The attacks that we have seen that get headlines every other day are often 15-year-olds in their basement, so it sort of creates a concern in our minds that we have a pretty big gap here, so certainly at Tripwire we have talked about this at a strategic level, and we are very supportive of, in fact pretty involved already with a number of governmental agencies in several different areas, certainly from more of a tactical standpoint in terms of providing them products and capabilities and services and so on, but also from a strategic standpoint there is some extremely good work going on between private industry and government around digital fingerprinting and understanding the security and stability of computer systems at a very fundamental level, and the National Drug Intelligence Agency and many other agencies have been positively involved in that.

So we are starting to see the kind of activity that is moving, I think, the nation to a higher level of overall security, but it worries us that it is not moving as quickly as it probably could or should, and so we certainly welcome additional leadership from you and your bills in those areas.

Senator WYDEN. Mr. Logan, let us have you comment on this as well. You have got an innovative technology, a product out there that you are excited about, that you think makes sense. You have spent a lot of time toiling away on it, but you are not exactly sure where in government to bring it. What Senator Allen and I have said is, you could bring it to a clearinghouse within NIST. That would be where you would go, and the clearinghouse would basically share that information with an agency that expresses a need.

Now, that is our sort of bipartisan thinking about how you could streamline this and build on something that we think would not involve a lot of red tape and bureaucracy. Do you by and large feel that is heading in the right direction?

Mr. LOGAN. Yes, I do. In fact, our current process of trying to evaluate new technology standards, the mechanics of that would be a federal government, state government, local government. It can be very cumbersome and time-consuming only to, at the end, to make a decision or arrive at a certain standards level, and now the technology has passed us by.

I believe that through a clearinghouse as you have suggested, that would give companies a chance to bring to the table innovative products, see how do they meet the needs of the users, today's needs of the users in a way that could help through enabling grantees to look to these various test beds, to say, well, it works for them, this is our need, our needs are aligned with the test beds, and to make that a part, to enable these grants—I mean, the big concern, obviously, with the user groups is, what are the mechanics associated with the grants that will be coming out, and so to the degree that we can show and demonstrate products and technologies that will enable first responders to better do their job, I think that is absolutely the way to go.

Senator WYDEN. Well, our hope is that taken together the test bed and the clearinghouse would really accelerate the adoption of new technology by government emergency and security agencies. Again, we would welcome your ideas on some of the specifics about how to address this, but I would hope that we could get agreement on those two areas, because I am struck by how many times private sector companies say, "Look, I do not know where to turn." Clearly there is a governmental interest at a minimum in not buying outdated stuff, and making sure that when you are making these purchases, that you are buying in a cost-effective way for citizens and taxpayers.

Just a couple of other areas, one for you, Mr. Logan, with respect to the wireless area, which we do think is especially important. Our hope is that the pilot program that we envisage would be a helpful start. Clearly, this is going to require some very significant expenditures.

There are some exciting things going on around the country, as Mr. Starnes noted, where he is involved in some of them in the State of Oregon, in my home state, but our theory is that we could provide grants to states to at least pioneer some innovative efforts and communications interoperability, and these could be shared around the country. We see that as one way to at least make a start and jump-start the effort to come up with some good models. Are you comfortable that is headed in the right direction?

Mr. LOGAN. Yes. I think that is a very good idea, especially working with States that may have already made significant advances in the area of interoperable technology, communications improvements. In fact, a thought we had was in working with these test beds, maybe creating a solution whereby we can not only demonstrate the technologies at that location, but put those technologies on the road in a mobile setting much like FEMA and others, first responders.

Usually the event is not going to happen, maybe, right next door or where they think it is going to happen, but if we can develop through those test beds the ability to have those solutions mobile so we can bring them to various communities in other states, I think that could be very beneficial.

Senator WYDEN. Another area, last area that we were interested in that goes back to S. 2182, and maybe we can start with you, Dr. Strawn, is, I think the theory of this bill is to buildup what has been certainly heretofore an underdeveloped intellectual infrastructure in the cyber security field. Take your academic hat off for a moment, and give me your thoughts on what you think the practical effects of underinvestment, what is happening now, the current underinvestment in cyber security research and personnel would be.

Dr. STRAWN. I think underinvestment has put us in somewhat of a pickle already, and that the citizens of our country are right not to have trust in their computing and information technology systems.

We do not have a high enough level of assurance that our systems are safe from being hijacked, are safe from being abused; and now computer hardware and computer software are going into almost all products and services that society uses these days. We just have to have a higher level of security and a higher level of reliability in these systems, and the public will have to remain doubtful until we take it to a higher level.

Senator WYDEN. Gentlemen, anybody else, practical effects of underinvestment?

Dr. HOFFMAN. Following up on those earlier comments, I would only add that we have a system where the critical infrastructures are all connected, so in fact what affects computing does not only affect computing. Computing drives energy and water and a number of other infrastructures more and more, so if we do not have secure computing systems, we really do not have a secure infrastructure at all, and it just gets worse as a practical effect.

Also, I would like to followup on one comment made a minute ago. When you talk about a test bed, I think it is important to realize—and I agree with the observation that these things can more and more be taken on the road, so you do not need a big lab with lots of rooms out at NIST or somewhere else. The people nowadays come and ask at the university, they say, let us see your lab, and I say, well, where do you want me to bring it, because often for many systems three laptops and a good mobile wireless network is all you need to demonstrate something, and you have much more of an effect when it is there in the right place.

Senator WYDEN. I think that is a very good point. I was concerned initially when we started talking about the strategic technology reserve people would think about some gigantic building, and there you would store all of these laptops, and they would just be getting dusty and the like, and then you would have your test bed, which would be a similar sort of building hooked up to all kinds of jumper cables and contraptions, and that would be supposed to be in charge of testing.

I think you are absolutely right. What we are looking at is trying to use existing laboratories and others to the greatest extent possible, and we are going to take that counsel to heart. I am glad you made that point, because I think people are already starting to envisage how this would work, and it is helpful to have this kind of testimony on the record.

Others on that, underinvestment?

Mr. STARNES. I cannot resist that one. I think we are actually seeing first-hand the practical effect of underinvestment right now. Customers have been taught to buy based on features, and the number of colors on their screen and other issues, and have not really been taught to understand the issues of security and interconnectedness and various other important areas for infrastructure, so the commercial instincts kick in, which is a part of our democratic process, so somehow we have to find a balance, and sort of back to the issue of test bed clearinghouse again, which is a concept we certainly endorse.

The key issue, a couple of the key issues that distinguish the commercial sector from the government sector is speed, so not only does the funding have to be allocated both in terms of internal budgets for agencies, but it has to be made available, and it has to be made available, as I said in my oral testimony, on a faster basis than we currently have the ability to do. That certainly does impact commercial entities, because commercial entities are forced to go out to the venture capital market, and when the venture capital market is strong, as it has been over the last few years, that was a viable option.

The fact of the matter is now that the venture capital markets for the most part are weak, and so you are actually seeing a decline of commercial innovation, and government really has not stepped forward in our view to really deal with that yet.

Senator WYDEN. Well, I really do not have any questions in addition. You all have been excellent, and my hope is that these two bills can, in effect, provide a very solid response to what happened on September 11, and really constitute a new and more targeted effort by government to deal with cyber security issues and the threats that were presented on September 11.

It seems to me with the cyber security legislation that passed the House, we have got a chance to make a very effective and well-targeted investment in NIST and the National Science Foundation, and ensuring that we are training tomorrow's leaders. That is essentially what that legislation is all about.

I support it strongly, and the Administration's efforts in that area with respect to S. 2037. I think what we would like to say is that while government clearly can make a very significant difference, it would just be a tragedy not to harness and mobilize all of this energy and talent in the private sector that wants to help and pitch-in and make a difference. I am convinced that over the next month, working closely with the Administration, and with all of you in the private sector, we can move this forward.

There are not many months left in this session of Congress, and I think it would be a real shame to go home without passing these two bills, bills that are going to allow us to maximize an effective role of tax dollars, particularly in education and research, and a small amount of additional government money basically to ensure that the volunteers and people in science and IT who want to help can have a chance to do so and make a difference.

So, if there is nothing that any of you would like to add further, we will adjourn, but I can give each of you the last crack. Anything that our panel would like to add?

[No response.]

Senator WYDEN. All right. We are adjourned.

[Whereupon, at 4:15 p.m., the Subcommittee adjourned.]

APPENDIX

PREPARED STATEMENT OF JAMES W. GRAHAM, CHIEF OPERATING OFFICER, EMERGENCY ASSET MANAGEMENT SYSTEMS

Mr. Chairman, Members of the Committee, thank you for this opportunity to submit testimony in support of S. 2037, the Science and Technology Emergency Mobilization Act.

My name is James W. Graham, Chief Operating Officer of Emergency Asset Management System, a division of GBUCS, LLC. GBUCS is a Chicago-based developer of web-based software solutions for private industry and government, specializing in asset management systems.

I am here today to express our strong support for S. 2037.

Overseas, our Armed Forces are unbeatable not only because of their training, patriotism and bravery, but also because they are equipped with unsurpassed technological superiority. Here on the home front—where terrorism must be fought and the safety of our communities and workplaces ensured—we too must equip ourselves with unsurpassed homeland security technology.

In recent months, our company has dedicated itself to learning about the technology needs of emergency managers nationwide. Based on our experience I must report to you that there are serious and substantial shortcomings in the technologies now utilized by emergency management agencies. Much has been said about the need to make communications systems between emergency response agencies interoperable. Technology needs on the home front do not stop there.

Emergency managers at every level of government in this country are certified and dedicated professionals who typically graduate to their important positions after gaining experience in the military, on police forces and as firefighters. These federal, state and local agencies play a critical role in responding to terrorist attacks. They coordinate and mobilize all available regional, state and federal assets in times of disaster. These include police, fire, National Guard, hazardous materials units, public health and infectious disease professionals, volunteers, donors and many others. Little noticed when there is no emergency, these emergency response professionals took on critical importance when terrorists struck Oklahoma City, New York, Washington and elsewhere. They will play such roles again, and we must equip them with the best tools and technologies available.

Seven months after September 11, 2001, many of these emergency managers remain under funded, understaffed and unequipped with the technology they need. State government budgets took a direct hit when the economy crashed, and as much as state legislators and governors wish to invest in homeland security, they often lack the means to do so.

To illustrate one of the gaps we discovered, consider that emergency management agencies make little or no use of Internet technologies even though their central function is to gather critical information in emergencies and communicate instructions to needed emergency responders. In other words, although information management and communications is central to their role, they make almost no use of the Internet, the greatest information and communications invention of the past century.

In several disasters of the past decade, people by the thousands who wanted to volunteer had to try to get through on the phone; there were no web sites to visit with instructions and information gathering capabilities. On September 11th, 15,000 unsolicited volunteers showed up in Manhattan, forcing authorities to help feed and shelter them. In other disasters, people who wanted to donate filled truckloads and even jumbo jets with unneeded goods, leaving emergency responders with the added burden of sorting through or disposing of inappropriate donations. No web site told donors what was needed nor was the web used to facilitate the logistics of moving and warehousing donations. Public confidence in the official disaster response was thus undermined. No private business facing similar logistical challenges would think of doing so without Internet tools of some kind.

A National Emergency Technology Guard would be an important and useful added force in guarding against terrorist attacks here at home. Technology professionals across the country will be willing to volunteer in an emergency. We ourselves volunteered and donated our own donations management software to the Manhattan Chamber of Commerce for use after September 11th. They have found it useful as they help businesses recover from that disaster.

A Center for Civilian Homeland Security Technology Evaluation would help identify needs and solutions such as those I have pointed out here today.

But state and local emergency managers need help now. If the federal government is to lend that helping hand, let there be money in the palm of that hand. Volunteer programs like a NET Guard and Citizen Corps can do great good, but they must be managed at the local and state level. That costs money and it requires logistical management tools they do not now have.

In times like these, the states lack the financial might of the federal government. But the strength of our defense against domestic terrorism depends upon the might of state and local emergency managers. They need new technology to be effective, and they need financial backing to acquire those technologies.

We support S. 2037, but we also call upon you to do more for those who are at the front line of terrorism defense at the state and local level. Thank you.

April 8, 2002

Hon. RON WYDEN,
Chairman,
Hon. GEORGE ALLEN,
Ranking Minority Member,
Senate Committee on Commerce, Science, and Transportation,
Subcommittee on Science, Technology, and Space,
Washington, DC.

Dear Chairman Wyden and Senator Allen:

The National Association of Manufacturers (NAM) writes to support your new legislation, S. 2037, the Science and Technology Emergency Mobilization Act (or NETGuard bill). The NAM is the nation's largest industrial trade association and represents 14,000 members (including 10,000 small and mid-sized companies) and 350 member associations serving manufacturers and employees in every industrial sector and all 50 states.

Homeland security is an area of significant new endeavor for the NAM in 2002. Governor Ridge, General Magaw and Representative Chambliss have addressed NAM audiences, including the NAM Board of Directors. Furthermore, the NAM has dedicated a major new segment of its Web site to the issue.

Your legislation would afford an organized way for industry to express its support, and to channel its involvement, in the homeland security effort. Even without such legislation, many U.S. firms, including many NAM-member companies, rushed to offer assistance in numerous ways following the terrorist attacks of September 11th. As encouraging as that response was, a greater degree of organization in the future can be expected to make industry contributions even more effective.

Among other provisions, the bill also would create a new unit at the National Institute of Standards and Technology to evaluate new technologies for their applications to homeland security and to serve as a clearinghouse. The NAM recently wrote to the director of NIST to call attention to a NIST project that we believe has higher homeland security-relevance than was previously appreciated. Our experience suggests, again, that a formal structure for such evaluations is a worthwhile idea.

David Peyton would be pleased to provide further information at (202) 637–3147.

Sincerely,

FRANKLIN J. VARGO,
Vice President, International Economic Policy.

April 19, 2002

Hon. RON WYDEN,
Chairman,
Senate Commerce, Science, and Transportation Committee,
Science, Technology and Space Subcommittee,
Washington, DC.

Dear Mr. Chairman:

The National Association of Manufacturers wishes to express its support for S. 2182, your cyber security research legislation. We strongly supported the counterpart legislation, H.R. 3394, as passed by the House of Representatives with 400 votes. The National Association of Manufacturers (NAM) is the nation's largest industrial trade association. The NAM represents 14,000 members (including 10,000 small and mid-sized companies) and 350 member associations serving manufacturers and employees in every industrial sector and all 50 states.

Since 1998, the NAM has led the effort to increase industry support for science funding generally, given the need to maintain the flow of new discoveries upon which industry can carry out product and process development, the need to produce more U.S. graduates in technical fields, and the need to defend the country against attack, including cyber attack. The NAM supported the broad research authorization bills issuing from this subcommittee (S. 2217, S. 296, S. 2046) that the Senate passed three times by unanimous consent starting in 1998. Today, the NAM is pleased to support the new specific bill, S. 2182, which addresses the most important topic not included in previous legislation: computer security.

The sobering hearing held by the House Science Committee last October 10, to be supplemented by your hearing on April 24, afforded evidence for the need for the legislation. Too little money is going into computer security research, too few graduates are being produced, and too little progress is being made. Computer users remain almost totally reliant on passive defenses such as virus filters and firewalls that afford no meaningful defense against distributed denial of service (DDOS) attacks. At Carnegie-Mellon University, the Computer Emergency Response Team's statistics on reported attacks show that malicious attacks are doubling annually, to a rate of over 50,000. Even the NAM itself, as a small business, receives about ten attempts at penetration each day.

The NAM views S. 2182 as one important piece of an evolving strategy to bring together the joint strengths of government, industry, and academe to meet the undeniable shared threat of cyber attack, along with the pending Critical Infrastructure Information Security Act, S. 1456. S. 2182 will have our support as it moves forward.

Sincerely,

FRANKLIN J. VARGO,
Vice President, International Economic Policy.

RESPONSE TO WRITTEN QUESTIONS SUBMITTED BY HON. JOHN MCCAIN TO DR. GEORGE STRAWN

Question 1. One concern that has been raised about S. 2182 is that many of the grants established by this program will be used to develop evolutionary technologies, such as a next generation firewall. How does NSF plan to ensure that it funds research programs that are truly revolutionary?

Answer. "Evolutionary" and "revolutionary" are terms often associated with research proposals. They can be thought of as the ends of a spectrum of research contributions ranging from "pure" evolutionary (only a modest or incremental increase in understanding is likely to occur from undertaking the proposed research) through various blends of "part evolutionary, part revolutionary", to "pure revolutionary" (a very large increase in understanding, often in unexpected directions, is proposed). The other side of the same coin is proposal risk. If only incremental understanding is sought, reviewers can be relatively sure that the proposer will be successful (i.e., the proposal is of lower risk). On the other hand, if large increases in understanding are sought, the reviewers will be less sure that the proposer will succeed (i.e., the proposal is of higher risk). When scientists speak of "the quality" of a proposed research project, part of the determination of quality is how revolutionary the proposed project appears to be.

NSF selects proposals for funding by merit review. Usually this merit review includes proposal review by scientific experts familiar with the subject material of the proposal. The review focuses on two questions: what is the scientific merit of the proposed research? And what are the broader implications of the proposed research?

The NSF program officer in charge of the review then makes awards as possible, utilizing the advice of the expert reviewers. At all stages of the NSF proposal process, revolutionary research is sought. Proposers are told that NSF is interested in funding revolutionary research; reviewers are encouraged by NSF to regard revolutionary proposals highly during the peer review; and program officers are encouraged by NSF to "take the chance" on higher risk, revolutionary proposals while making their funding decisions. All of these steps are intended to counter tendencies along the process to lower risks by settling for more evolutionary proposals with higher probabilities of success. One implication of this is that if some proposals funded by NSF don't fail, we aren't taking big enough risks.

Question 2. A number of different federal agencies, include the NSF, NIST, and DoD all fund cyber security projects. Is there a guiding organization or established working group that shares information about federal cyber security research and will ensure that the grant and research programs established by this bill will not fund duplicative research?

Answer. There is an interagency organization, the Networking and Information Technology Research and Development working group (NITRD), which includes the federal agencies supporting IT research. This working group has been in existence for more the ten years and has a history of providing excellent coordination among the various federal IT research programs. NITRD is under the auspices of OSTP and OMB.

Question 3. You have testified that "the most important problem" in cyber security research is that there is such a small number of faculty doing research in this field.

a) What created this shortage?

b) Do you believe S. 2182 will reduce this shortage and increase the number of faculty involved in this field?

c) Is the shortage of Ph.D's and graduates in the cyber security research area any worse than in other engineering and science fields?

Answer. It is a matter of speculation as to why the cohort of researchers working in the cybersecurity area is so small. One clear cause is that until very recently (coinciding with the rise in the use of the Internet) very few organizations worried about cybersecurity. In the absence of identification of serious, challenging problems, hardly any faculty chose to work in the area, meaning that almost no new researchers were produced.

Researchers choose their areas of study based on personal interest, funding availability, and various other reasons. Perhaps the academic values that include "free and open access to information" have been at odds with the "secure and controlled access to information" requirements of cybersecurity research. Perhaps there just hasn't been enough funding available. For example, NSF funding levels in various areas are often determined in a bottom up fashion (by so-called "proposal pressure"). In any event, increasing the amount of research funding is an important and usually successful way increasing the number of researchers working in an area.

Additional disincentives to working in security include the fact that until recently the only employer was the Department of Defense, so it is likely that many academic advisors did not encourage their students to go into this area. In the private sector, employers are interested in program features, not security.

In FY02, NSF initiated a program in cybersecurity (called "Trusted Computing") and one result has been an increase in the number of cybersecurity proposals received by NSF. The shortage of computer scientists working and trained in high-demand areas such as cybersecurity and networking is greater than in some traditional areas such as programming languages and operating systems. Other areas of science and engineering exhibit a similar variation between high-demand and lower-demand sub areas.

Question 4. You stated that cyber security is a property of the "total system," not of the system components, which includes human and management elements.

Do you believe that the bill, S. 2182, as introduced, does an adequate job of providing funding for this "total system" approach? Is there a need for additional multidisciplinary research in this area?

Answer. Cybersecurity is a system characteristic, not a component characteristic. This means that researchers have to study the interrelationships among system components as well as the components themselves. Since, broadly speaking, some of the system components are humans and organizations interdisciplinary research arises naturally in this area. S. 2182 addresses these needs because the researchers (and NSF and other federal agencies) are well aware of these characteristics. NSF strives to be as general as possible in its program announcements and solicitations because many of the best proposal ideas "bubble up" from the research community itself as opposed to being specified in the announcement. Once an area such as cybersecurity is marked for additional support, over specification can deter, rather than enhance community proposal response.

Question 5. You mentioned the research and other education programs that NSF is currently conducting. Can NSF conduct the type of research and education activities called for in the Cyber Security Research and Development Act within their existing statutory authority?

Answer. We believe that the research and education called for in S. 2182 can be supported (and indeed is already being supported) within NSF's current statutory authority.

Question 6. Your written testimony highlighted the NSF's Cybercorps program, which provides scholarships to undergraduate and graduate students studying computer security and in return the students will serve in the federal government for a least two years. Have you had any problems placing students of the Cybercorps program into summer internships positions within the federal government?

Answer. The Federal Cyber Service: Scholarship for Service (SFS) program has placed more than 24 students in internships in various federal agencies this past summer—the first such opportunity provided for students within the program. As in any new undertaking, there have been challenges associated with (a) moving awareness that SFS students are available for internships beyond agency personnel offices to various agencies, (b) achieving understanding that though these students are available for less than 640 hours of employment in a summer, they may be still be incorporated within existing agency provisions for Federal Student Career Experience Program, and (c) overcoming agency concerns that though they may go through a very expensive clearance process, students are not committed to service only within the federal agency within which they have served their internship. The Office of Personnel Management is the lead agency addressing these issues and is working with the hiring agencies, and the grantees institutions to resolve these issues.

Question 7. On April 22, Matt Bishop, a computer science professor at the University of California—Davis, and Blaine Burnham, founding director of the Nebraska University Consortium on Information Assurance, detailed concerns about the Cybercorps program at the Infotec 2002 Conference.

One criticism raised by these speakers is that government salaries are so low that students prefer to apply for student loans and repay them with private industry jobs instead of joining the Cybercorps program. Another critique of other science-targeted scholarship programs is that students with federal scholarships are able to get out of service requirements, because private companies will re-pay the scholarship as part of their employment package. What has NSF done with the Cybercorps program to attract students to the program and ensure that students that receive scholarships under the program will actually perform the required government service?

Another criticism that was raised by the speakers is that graduates of the Cybercorps program are required to only work for civilian agencies. The speakers recommended that graduates of the program be allowed to work for the Department of Defense and its research agencies. What is NSF's position on this recommendation?

Answer. Working through its grantees, NSF has been very active in increasing awareness of the program and its requirements. We have been gratified by the level of press attention devoted to the program and the student interest as demonstrated by direct inquiries to NSF. The program's requirements are explicitly communicated to our grantee institutions and, through them, to participating students. Although the criticisms about low government salaries and private industry options may be valid, they are not widespread. In fact, we have noted an enthusiastic response on the part of participating students. The main deterrence here is in the recruitment of students with the proper mindset and attitude about federal service.

The vast majority of students currently enrolled in SFS are not planning to make a lot of money in private industry job by abusing a government scholarship program. On the contrary, they are in SFS because they sincerely want to give back to America and contribute to the ongoing war on terrorism. They are motivated by patriotism and a desire to serve in much the same way that young people volunteer for military service. This is the attitude frequently expressed by the student participants, drawn from among all grantee institutions, at the recent Cybercorps Symposium held July 20–24, 2002 at the University of Tulsa.

In order to avoid unnecessary duplication with a similar program being run by the National Security Agency (NSA) which provides placement in Department of Defense agencies, NSF would like to see its SFS graduates be placed at federal civilian agencies. However, we do currently permit SFS graduates to be placed at DoD agencies and have done so. NSA and the U.S. Air Force—Rome Laboratory already have SFS graduates placed there and the Defense Computer Forensic Laboratory is scheduled to receive an intern.

Question 8. In your written testimony, you stated that "one important goal of fundamental long term research in cyber security will be to produce an agreement on what . . . constitutes a secure system." Could you please discuss why it so hard to reach an agreement on this issue, and what factors are involved in determining a "secure system"

Answer. The definition of a "secure system" depends on "how big" a system is being considered (see answer to question 4). That is, if the personnel who operate the computers and networks are thought of as part of the system, then cybersecurity melds with physical security, and issues of insider crime, etc, must be considered. And as with any discussion of security, perfection is not available and we must come to terms with levels of risk. Measuring risk in the computers and networks of a big system is a newer challenge, and less well understood than risk in pre-cyber systems.

Question 9. In your view, how vulnerable is the United States to the threat of cyber attack? Do we currently have the resources to prevent and respond to a cyber attack?

Answer. Research organizations such as NSF may not be in the best position to evaluate the current threat levels or response and prevention capabilities of the U.S. to cyber attack. Nevertheless, it can be said that today's cybersystems are poorly understood and poorly constructed relative to desired scientific and engineering standards. It is the goal of research to achieve better understanding of cybersystems and to create better engineering approaches for constructing such systems

Question 10. Would you consider America as a leader in cyber security research? If not, which countries are?

Answer. The U.S. remains the world leader in IT research and development, including cybersecurity. In cybersecurity, however, there is much to be learned and to be applied to a society increasingly dependent on computer technology. In some areas of cybersecurity, Israel is very advanced and may actually lead the U.S., due, perhaps, to their long-time need for security.

○

APEX
TP
9780160733062
76901945 – 46